Good enough

NIKKI HEYDER

Good enough

THE
DREAMWORK
COLLECTIVE

A ROADMAP FOR COMPASSIONATE SELF-ACCEPTANCE

This edition was published by The Dreamwork Collective

The Dreamwork Collective LLC, Dubai, United Arab Emirates

thedreamworkcollective.com

Printed and bound in the United Arab Emirates
by Al Ghurair Printing and Publishing LLC
Cover and design: Kasia Piatek, kasiapiatek.pl

Text © Nikki Heyder, 2024

ISBN 978-9948-742-91-3

Approved by the National Media Council Dubai, United Arab Emirates
MC-02-01-4127022

Good enough

A ROADMAP FOR COMPASSIONATE SELF-ACCEPTANCE

Table of Contents

This book is dedicated to any person who has ever felt not good enough... I think that includes all of us, right?

Introduction

I remember thinking to myself, *They don't mean it. They're just trying to be nice.* Perhaps it's a thought you've also had whenever someone has complimented you or congratulated you for something you have achieved.

It's always fascinated me why we do this. Why we cringe when someone says something nice to us, or why we want to run away and hide when we are celebrated.

Why do so many of us harbour shame and "not enoughness"? Why, when we are complimented, do we quickly find a way to prove it to be wrong?

These questions formed the basis for this book. The subject is something I have been actively researching and understanding throughout my years of practice as a therapist.

I'm assuming it sparks your curiosity, too, which might be why you were drawn to this book in the first place. Perhaps you also are in constant battle with yourself. Perhaps you are more familiar than you'd like to be with that loud, critical voice within you that constantly reminds you that you're "not good enough". Perhaps you want to release the pressure you place on yourself in your quest for validation, acceptance, or to simply just fit in.

Many people have asked me why I chose to write on this topic. My answer? Because I think it's something that everyone struggles with to some extent. Every client I have ever worked with struggles with their feelings of not being enough in some way. In fact, I don't really know how a person *wouldn't* struggle with it to some degree. I say this simply because it's part of human nature to long for connection, attachment, and belonging and therefore it's inevitable that we have a fear of *not* belonging.

I have watched how the inner critic antagonises a person until their anxiety completely cripples them. Where their fear of judgement becomes so great that they decide they're happier settling for loneliness than potentially meeting a new companion. I've watched how our not-good-enough statements lead us to addiction (of all kinds). I have seen how our lack of understanding of who we are in situations, relationships, friendships, and life circumstances is ultimately harmful to us.

I think that this innate fear is, in essence, a form of perfectionism. And not in the sense that we all want to be "perfect" per se but rather that all people who have perfectionistic tendencies harbour some sort of fear around their not-enoughness, whether it be fear of failure, fear of judgement, fear of being fully seen by another, or fear of abandonment and rejection. Perfectionism wears many hats and comes in all different shapes and sizes. It can be present in one area of your life and completely absent in another.

The research shows that perfectionistic tendencies have not only significantly increased over the years but that they are also correlated with a high risk of anxiety, depression, and suicidal ideation. Now, you may be thinking, *But I'm not a perfectionist*, and I want to clarify here that in the context of these pages, I refer to a perfectionist as anyone who feels inherently as though they're not enough in one way or another.

Before we go any further, take a moment to identify whether any of the following statements resonate for you.

* You feel shame around your personality, your body, or your voice.
* You are forever comparing your life/body/ relationship/career to everyone else's.
* You know you have an unhealthy, emotionally charged relationship with food (or other substances/behaviours).
* You no longer want to use external means as an emotional escape or control mechanism.
* You're tired of being bullied by your own inner critic.
* You want to stop procrastinating with everything you do.
* You want to take on opportunities in your life instead of saying no out of fear of failure.

* You no longer want to feel resentment from having your boundaries crossed by others (and yourself).
* You are ready to let go of the anxiety that comes from every social interaction.
* You really, truly, genuinely want to understand who you are.
* You crave peace, freedom, and a sense of belonging.

I belong to myself and I am enough.

If you caught yourself nodding your head to any of those points, then I want you to make me one promise, okay? That you will give your absolute best at being committed, present, and open to the idea that it can all change.

But before we delve into the good stuff, let me introduce myself.

My name is Nikki Heyder, and I am a holistic psychotherapist (which means I use a variety of modalities to help my clients through their struggles), a coach and mentor to fellow space holders, a former clinical nutritionist, and a therapeutic yoga teacher... And did I mention I'm someone who really questioned my own self-worth for a very long time?

I have worked for over a decade within the wellness space and pursued my studies in counselling psychology because of the types of patients I was treating as a nutritionist. These women were burnt out, chronically stressed, obsessive yo-yo dieters, or, even worse, stuck in the grasp of an eating disorder. They didn't need new meal plans, or even diet advice for that matter. What they needed was someone to understand them, show them compassion, and give them permission to get their mind out of societal expectations, to let go of the grip of their inner critic, to stop shaming themselves, and to start living life on their own terms. These women believed that to be loved or accepted they needed to look a certain way, or they were so stressed out, burnt out, anxious, or depressed, that they turned to food (either in bingeing and purging, or through starvation) as a means to find temporary relief from their emotional discomfort.

Battling your not-good-enough mindset isn't just about the pressure you place on your appearance. It could be about the pressure you place on yourself regarding your idea of success, money, status, relationships, or the way you socialise. At the core of your scramble for perfection is fear, insecurity, indecisiveness, and a deep conditioning that has led you to believe that who you are, as you are, is not worthy. This fear is usually accompanied by the emotion of shame.

Since becoming a therapist, I have had the privilege of working at a drug and alcohol rehabilitation clinic and seeing just how far shame can take us. As much as it broke my heart to see the damage caused by long-term use of substances, I could also understand that these substances played an important role in helping these people find a sense of temporary relief, peace, control, and even brief moments of belonging—things they craved but never received as children.

Now, you might not be deep into substance abuse or battling with an eating disorder, but you don't need to be in order to be worthy of doing the work of personal development and healing. Oftentimes, the perfectionist within us comes out in the subtlest of ways: the social anxiety, the not speaking up when we want to, the settling for an emotionally abusive partner, the emotional exhaustion of people-pleasing, the inability to set boundaries.

I created this book because as I reflected on the hundreds of people I have supported over the years, I realised that there was a process involved in the journey toward true self-acceptance. I wanted to share a simple four-step process for rewriting your definition of perfection and for normalising your "shame story". Trust me, we all have one. How this shows up behaviourally will differ for each of us. It may look like being an overachiever *or* hiding from the world. It could mean being a workaholic *or* being stuck in paralysis and doing nothing. We either believe that if we *just* do or don't do that one thing, then life will finally fall into place. The behaviour or symptoms we see on the outside can vary vastly depending on the person and their lived experiences and internal beliefs. But what I've come to realise is that at the root of it all, when you really dig deep, it usually stems from a similar wound of fear and shame.

So where does this wound come from, and why does it affect so many of us? The desire to be loved, accepted, and understood for who we authentically are is a shared human experience. Unfortunately, for a variety of reasons that we will explore in this book, many of us haven't truly experienced what it's like to be loved, accepted, and understood. The steps outlined in this book are the result of me working with hundreds of people just like you, as well as going through my own share of trial and error in my personal quest for cultivating greater self-compassion and self-acceptance.

I have been sucked into the comparison trap of wishing and wanting a life that never aligned with my actual values. I chose toxic, abusive partners in a desperate attempt to heal my inner wounds with my father. I have many limiting beliefs around being "stupid", which is why, regardless of my accomplishments, I often still battle with imposter syndrome. Take, for instance, right now as I write this book. Here's a snapshot of what my inner critical voice is saying: *Who am I to be writing a book? Who will even listen to me? Who do I think I am to be some kind of expert on this topic? This is going to be a complete flop.* Part of me cringes even thinking about it. Yet there's also a part of me who recognises the critical voice now and who understands that she exists because she is scared and she wants to keep me safe. I recognise that I have a choice to either listen to her and *not* publish this book, or listen to my heart and my intuition and find the courage to do it anyway.

As well as my own internal battles of not-enoughness, I also know how shame and low self-worth plays out in other people's lives because it's what I do, day in, day out. In my office I listen to people sharing their deepest fears and darkest thoughts. And I have the honour of supporting them as we navigate it together with tenderness and compassion. All I can offer through this book is my own perspective and, hopefully, a simple and straightforward way to help you climb out of the cage that has your authenticity trapped. My hope is that slowly but surely it will give you the permission and the courage to spread your wings and find freedom of self, just as I have seen happen with many others.

One thing I know for sure is that for most of us, when we understand *why* something is the way it is and how it applies to our unique story, and when we can then bring compassion to that, we feel almost immediate relief. And that's what I hope for you by the time you finish this book. That you develop the skill of being able to look at yourself and your life through compassionate eyes. That you can zoom out and see where change can be made and where acceptance must be embodied to finally feel at peace.

People need to understand what's going on beneath the surface. Yes, you might have limiting beliefs or self-harming behaviours, but *why*? If we don't understand the mechanisms of why something is happening, it becomes too easy to turn a blind eye or not do the work. Ignorance is bliss... or so they say.

Like the 12 Steps of Recovery, the first part of any change is the (often difficult) admission that we are facing a challenge we cannot solve ourselves. So, well done on completing that step. Your purchase of this book is you announcing to yourself that you are ready for a change. The second part is developing the *willingness* to embark on the sometimes difficult and confronting journey of self-inquiry.

That's where this book commences. These pages consist of a simple four-step approach to self-acceptance. These are the four steps:

Step 1: Awareness both of yourself and how your behaviours and symptoms limit your life, as well as awareness of how your lived experiences impact your belief systems.

Step 2: Understanding of how these beliefs then turn into "symptoms" and behaviours that may not necessarily serve you well.

Step 3: Reconnection to your authentic nature through practices of re-parenting work, compassion, forgiveness, acceptance, and respect.

Step 4: Action of taking everything you now know about yourself and how you wish to change and finally moving toward inner peace and self-acceptance.

If you are willing and open to do the work outlined in the following chapters (and you do them consistently regardless of setbacks and relapses), then I have no doubt that you will feel more empowered to

* finally let go of the anxiety and pressure of unreasonable expectations.
* stop comparing yourself to everything and everyone around you.
* learn how to accept yourself (and perhaps even love yourself) just as you are.
* understand your emotions and behaviours, without judgement.
* respect the function and purpose of your body and mind like never before.
* listen to and understand the signs and signals from your body.
* become articulate in the way you communicate your thoughts, feelings, and needs.
* get on your own side and become your own BFF.
* cultivate more meaningful relationships.

* be present with your life in each moment instead of wishing for something more.
* rewrite your shame story.
* honour your uniqueness.

How to Navigate This Book

My recommendation is that you read this book in order, from start to finish. Work through the steps one at a time and have a go at doing the associated mindfulness-based exercises, check-ins, and journal prompts that come with each lesson. Go slow. Take it all in. Take breaks. Reread parts if you need to. Take notes. I have tried to keep the contents of this book both informative and accessible. There will be parts you may want to research more, or parts that don't really pique your interest. Each person's journey is unique, so I give you full permission to take the parts that resonate the most for you.

Try to keep your journal prompts together in one notebook or document, and date them so you can revisit them in six months, one year, or even five years. Reflection is a wonderful way to track progress and growth.

Once you finish the book, feel free to reread the parts that resonated with you the most. Stay curious and open. You can use this book multiple times during different stages of your life. It'll hopefully become the catalyst for you to remember who you authentically are, whenever you find yourself feeling a little lost.

Step 1

Awareness

I t's hard to know what needs to change, or in which direction we need to head, without first having some awareness of what's showing up for us now, and of where it all started. Awareness is a skill you will learn how to fine tune throughout this book and is something you will keep refining year after year after year, the more you get to know yourself. The purpose of awareness is to broaden one's perspective, to be able to cast off the blinkers that often limit us. Becoming more aware means understanding concepts and theories and alternate viewpoints to your current ones. It means understanding others and what they may be experiencing at any given moment, and it means becoming more observant of who you are and how you operate in this life.

Imagine for a minute that you are a client of mine. You walk into my therapy room for the first time. After you get comfortable and we chitchat for a little bit, I will eventually ask you something like: "What brings you here today?" or "How do you know that you're in need of therapy?"

And you will come up with a response—some form of awareness and self-reflection around what's going well for you and what's not. You might say that you don't understand why you keep yelling at your partner or your kids when that's not the type of spouse or parent you truly wish to be. Or why every time you get home from a social gathering you beat yourself up about what you said or didn't say and assume that everyone is talking about you behind your back. Or how every time you get overwhelmed you isolate yourself and binge on wine or fast food when you know that it just makes you feel worse.

Becoming aware of yourself is indeed a superpower. I always tell my clients that self-awareness and awareness of where it all comes from is more than half the job done. Without awareness we can't change, right? Once we have awareness, we can tend to things differently, to choose a new path, a different behaviour, to take a pause. Awareness allows a person to be *responsive* to life rather

> Awareness allows a person to be *responsive* to life rather than *reactive* to it.

than *reactive* to it. In my opinion, this is one of, if not the most fundamental parts of healing. I like to refer to self-awareness as cultivating the skill of self-witnessing. The more we can observe ourselves without judgement, the more possibilities open up for us. The paradox is that self-witnessing is often the part people want to avoid because, initially, it can be the most painful. There is a beautiful quote by Rumi that states "the wound is the place where the light enters you". In other words, it's within these places and parts of ourselves that we avoid that offer us the greatest opportunity for transformation. To face these parts of ourselves means to truly embrace who we are and ultimately to turn our pain into wisdom.

Self-Reflection

I invite you now to try this self-reflection task and to think about your own life in the present moment.

* What do you do that doesn't align with your own moral compass?
* What do you wish was different and why?
* If you were to progress in your self-development, how would you know it's working? What would change or be different?

Self-awareness (and awareness in general) can be painful because it requires the acknowledgement of our current setbacks or stuck points, the admission of our wrongdoings, and ultimately of our past—our upbringing and our lived experiences, of remembering the moments of our lives that shaped our current beliefs and behaviours. As I mentioned previously, awareness also means becoming aware of certain concepts, theory, and terminology to make it all make sense. Without these foundational building blocks, the whole journey of self-development can feel much messier than it needs to be.

With that said, Steps 1 and 2 of this book are loaded with information. There is a lot of theory and a lot of different concepts to get your head around. It can feel like a great deal to take in, so I ask that you proceed with care. I always say to my clients that when we are exploring ourselves, never to do so with self-loathing or criticism but with curiosity and openness. The same goes with exploring your past. Don't look back with the intention of living there again, but rather to see it as an essential data collection exercise that holds many treasures or nuggets of wisdom that will lead you back to your authentic self.

If any of the lessons or journal prompts are triggering for you, make sure you have someone trustworthy to speak to, or better yet, work with a therapist of your own. Remember that you don't have to be a victim of your past if you choose not to be. Your past is a part of your history, but it doesn't have to define who you are now if you don't want it to. The truth is, you always have a choice in how you wish to show up in this world, but without awareness, you may not realise that's possible.

Lesson 1

Where It All Begins

If I had a dollar for the number of times people have said to me that therapy is just about blaming our parents for our current behaviours, I'd probably be a millionaire. And you know what? They're not entirely wrong. I don't like to blame people, though. I think we are responsible for ourselves, and blame only perpetuates self-pity, which ultimately doesn't get us very far.

But our childhood absolutely influences our thoughts, our beliefs, and therefore our actions. So, if we truly want to become aware of why we are the way we are, we can't not look at it. And this is what this lesson is all about: becoming aware of the influence of our early life experiences. Some of you may be rolling your eyes at this point or thinking, *My childhood was perfectly fine*, and if it was, that's great. But just remember that childhood doesn't have to be "bad" for it to have shaped our beliefs. *Everything* shapes our beliefs. Some for the better, and some for the worse. Sometimes it's merely the absence of something good that we didn't realise we needed that has a huge impact on our need for validation or lack of confidence now. Sometimes it's an observation of one of our caregivers' behaviours or insecurities (which probably stemmed from their own childhood experiences) that then shapes ours. Childhood experiences have such a significant impact because the brain is then in its most vulnerable stage of development, so quite literally, everything we experience shapes it in some way. This is just a fact.

I also suspect that many of you will be thinking, *I just can't remember much of my childhood, so how will this be relevant to me?*... and that's okay, too. You don't need to remember every detail.

What will help, though, is becoming aware of the environment in which you were raised. This means becoming aware of your physical surroundings (your home, your bedroom, your neighbourhood), your relationships (with caregivers, siblings, school friends), and how your emotions were tended to, how your needs were met, and how you developed your sense of self within that environment. Swiss psychologist and psychoanalyst Alice Miller states in her book, *The Drama of the Gifted Child,* that "Experience has taught us that we have only one enduring weapon in our struggle against mental illness: the emotional discovery and emotional acceptance of the truth in the individual and unique history of our childhood.".

Put simply, when you were born you obviously didn't have any lived experiences yet, which means *everything* you experience in those early years holds *so* much weight and *so* much meaning because, usually, it's the very first experience of that particular thing. Baby brains are like sponges, soaking up every experience and forming connections. And if something keeps happening over and over, those connections get stronger and stronger, shaping our beliefs about the world and ourselves.

Imagine a child who consistently receives warm, responsive care from their caregiver. They are held, soothed, and reassured whenever they cry or express discomfort. In this environment, the child learns to trust that their needs will be met and that they are worthy of love and attention. As they grow older, this belief in their own worthiness becomes deeply ingrained, shaping their interactions with others and their sense of self.

Now, contrast this with a child who experiences inconsistent or neglectful care. Perhaps their caregiver is frequently absent or emotionally unavailable, leaving the child feeling insecure and unsure of whether their needs will be met. In this environment, the child may develop beliefs that they are unworthy of love and attention, leading to challenges in forming healthy attachments and a persistent sense of inadequacy as they navigate relationships later in life.

In both cases, the early experiences of attachment profoundly influence the child's beliefs about their own worthiness and their ability to form secure attachments. These beliefs can have lasting effects, impacting their self-esteem, interpersonal relationships, and overall well-being throughout their life.

Although all babies are born with a unique temperament, it's the environment and the type of nurturing or conditioning a child receives that determines how that temperament develops over time.

Children have a few core primary needs. Physically, children require safety, food, sleep, shelter, and proper hygiene. They also require their emotional needs to be met, which enables them to develop a healthy sense of self. This means that they require their caregivers to provide them with things such as emotional safety, emotional attunement, connection (physical and emotional), acceptance and encouragement of their authentic expression, the active repair of relational ruptures when they arise, and loving discipline. If these are met, a healthy and secure attachment forms between child and caregiver, as does a healthy and secure sense of self.

I'm curious whether you can already identify a few key needs that may have been missing from your own upbringing.

When our core needs *aren't* met, we start to question our sense of self and our sense of belonging, which plants the seeds of doubt and shame in our minds. A well-known study referred to as the ACE study (Adverse Childhood Experiences) analysed the records of more than 17,000 everyday patients and found ten commonly reported adverse childhood experiences that predicted a range of psychological and medical issues within the adult.

These ten experiences are

- three kinds of abuse: sexual, physical, or emotional,
- two kinds of neglect: emotional or physical, and
- five kinds of household dysfunction: having separated or divorced parents, witnessing a mother or stepmother being treated violently, a household member addicted to alcohol or other substances, a household member who is suicidal or mentally unstable, and/or a household member in jail.

The more ACEs a person can tick off the list, the higher chance they have of developing physical symptoms such as coronary heart disease, asthma, and diabetes; mental health symptoms such as depression and anxiety; and health risk behaviours such as smoking, substance misuse, addiction, and physical inactivity.

What I find most interesting about child brain development, which is also noted in the ACE study, is that before the age of three years old, the parts of the brain associated with logic, reasoning, and language haven't really "turned on" yet. From the last trimester of pregnancy until approximately three years old, the dominant part of the brain is the part associated with one's felt sense of the world, implicit memory, and survival responses. In other words, it's the part of the brain that favours the connection to the body and intuition in response to safety or danger, as well as the limbic system, which is the part that regulates emotions. Interestingly, from sixteen weeks onward, a developing foetus can start to feel what the mother feels. Pretty cool, right? So up until the age of three we are feeling, sensing, and experiencing the world in a non-logical yet very impactful way. Even the memories we form during these early years are not explicit ones... they are implicit, associated with how we felt, rather than a specific time, date, or recount of events.

It's not uncommon for me to hear a client say something such as, "I know logically that I am not a bad person, but I *feel* like I am." This usually indicates to me that they are referring to their implicit memory. And what we know about implicit memories is that many of them are formed in early childhood.

The repetition of events and experiences in an infant and child's life will impact the strength of the synapses or neural connections within the brain, which essentially end up as the foundation of many of the beliefs we form about ourselves and the world. A child's brain develops extremely rapidly during the first 36 months of life. A process referred to as *blooming* explains how, by age two or three years old, a child has up to twice as many synapses as they will have in adulthood and that gradually, as the child becomes older, the "irrelevant" or weaker connections are slowly eliminated (often referred to as *pruning*). This blooming and pruning process shows us just how "plastic" the brain is, meaning that we aren't just born with a brain that feels and sees things a certain way. Rather, it grows and develops based on the experiences and input it receives and repeats the most. As the saying goes, "what fires together, wires together". Brain neurons that continuously respond to the same stimulus will become preferred connections, shaping the way we see ourselves and the world. For example, a child who learns that he or she must withhold their opinion in favour of not being ridiculed by their parent will grow up into an adult who, most likely, has the same default response in romantic relationships. Their brain has associated speaking up with being ridiculed and therefore learned that being quiet is the safest option. Any time in the future where they feel called to share their opinion, their brain will remember this pattern and employ the learned behaviour. Ongoing research on brain development proves time and time again just how impactful these early years are in cultivating secure, resilient, empathetic, and adaptable adults.

A client of mine (for confidentiality purposes let's name her Sarah) came to me a while ago wanting to work on her jealousy issues. Every time her partner interacted with another woman,

> The repetition of events and experiences in a child's life will impact the strength of the neural connections within the brain, which essentially end up as the foundation of many of the beliefs we form about ourselves and the world.

Sarah would feel angry and reactive, and they would end up in an argument. Once the argument was over, Sarah always felt remorseful and guilty that she had even questioned her partner's loyalty when she knows logically how much she trusts him. As we spent time exploring this pattern of hers, what became evident was that the behaviour toward her partner stemmed from her innate fear of betrayal and abandonment and her subsequent lack of trust in people close to her, due to her childhood experiences. Her father, who she was very close to, left her without saying goodbye when she was five years old. Her mother never helped her understand what happened and lied to her about the whole situation. As an only child, she felt she needed her mother close to her during this time of grief, but instead, her mother (who was inevitably also hurting) spent her nights with other men, which Sarah perceived as a betrayal of their connection. She felt as though her mother chose random men over her, which left her feeling not only physically abandoned, betrayed, and heart-broken by her father but also emotionally abandoned, betrayed, and heartbroken by her mother. The repetition of these small betrayals over time caused Sarah to develop her subconscious beliefs that anyone who loves her will leave her for "something better" and that who she is "isn't worthy." Once again, she knew she could trust her partner (who, by the way, proposed to her not long after our sessions and they are now happily married with a beautiful baby girl), but her felt sense of not being enough dictated her negative patterns. She would not have been able to understand that had she not gone through the self-inquiry process we undertook together.

As the logical part of the brain starts to develop more, we start making meaning out of everything and adapting our behaviours accordingly. We start to identify our sense of self-identity, how we fit into our environment, and how we attach to our caregivers. This conditioning process can create a huge shift in a person, pulling them far away from who they authentically are. If a child develops the belief that their authentic self is *not* a suitable fit for their surroundings, they will, through trial and error, adjust their personality and actions to better fit in. In other words, for many of us, there are parts of ourselves that we have suppressed for a long time in the fear that, if expressed, will cause a negative consequence. As you can imagine, this shapeshifting process can disconnect us from not only our authenticity but also our intuition.

The purpose of intuition is, in my opinion, to keep us alive and safe as well as to be a compass for our unique self-expression. It's like an inner guide who speaks on behalf of our authentic selves. We tend to forget as humans that we are very much still animals in many ways, and just like animals, we have the same innate sense of what is good and bad for us. It's our intuition that can sense if a person is dangerous, and it's also our intuition that tells us whether we prefer the colour blue over yellow. You'll know your intuition is speaking when you have that gut knowing: a grounding feeling within your belly or body.

Unfortunately, however, due to the conditioning process just explained, most of us get separated from our intuition at a very young age. We learn not to trust it because whenever we do, it seems to get us in trouble, or we get bullied, or ignored, or judged... Imagine that your intuition tells you as a six-year-old to wear your favourite pink leggings with a spiderman shirt. You arrive at school super happy with how you look, but instead of the other kids loving your choices, too, they laugh at you. Imagine your intuition tells you to ask a question at the dinner table because you don't understand the topic your father is discussing, and instead of explaining it to you kindly, he scoffs and says, "How stupid can you be?". Imagine your intuition guides you toward wanting to study primary school teaching, but when you excitably announce this to your family, they get angry at you for making a career choice with such low income. What happens to that voice within you? You shut it down, right? You don't want to trust it or listen to it because every time you do, you receive the message from others that you are wrong or bad. It's these types of experiences that cause that huge disconnect from your true nature and that leave many of us as adults feeling somewhat purposeless, as if there is some secret ingredient missing from our lives.

Self-Reflection

* What experiences do you think have shaped some of your innate feelings and beliefs about yourself or others?
* What are some of the beliefs you currently hold about yourself or others that you know aren't true but that you continue to believe anyhow?
* How does this affect your life and relationships?

We shut down our intuition purely to try and protect ourselves and prioritise our much-needed attachment early on in life. You see, attachment during infancy is crucial, regardless of whether that attachment is good for us in the long term. As babies and children, we are 100 percent dependent on our caregivers and the environment in which we are raised. We cannot fend for ourselves, feed ourselves, earn money, or navigate our medical requirements. This is especially true for the first eight years of life when we have only really just learned how to walk, talk, and conceptualise the outside world. What happens when our caregivers are not nurturing or well attuned to our needs and development?

All children will attempt to communicate their needs and wants in response to their intuition and inner knowing, be it a cuddle, to be fed, to go to sleep, or to have discomfort comforted. This expression will come from a felt sense of what's happening within the body, (otherwise known as *interoception*), as well as input from what's happening around the child (a process we call *neuroception*). A child might express their feelings or needs through crying or making noises, tearing up, throwing tantrums, sulking, and/or outwardly trying to seek attention in any way possible. Now this may come as a surprise to some (and as a parent it's easy to forget), but it's actually not up to the child to know exactly what's going on for them. It's up to the adult to become curious about the child's expression and to attune to that with understanding, love, and appropriate discipline/boundaries when necessary. If the child attempts to express themselves through any of these various ways and the caregiver ignores the child, punishes the child, belittles the child, mocks the child, or starts acting like a child themselves, the child will very quickly learn that it is not safe to be *authentic*. It is not safe to express their true needs and wants. It is not safe to show certain emotions. It is not safe to speak up about certain things. In other words, it's not safe to listen to their intuition. And so, understandably, they start to disconnect from themselves and find other behavioural coping mechanisms and personality traits that allow them to remain attached to their environment purely to survive and "fit in".

To recap: We as humans both *feel the world* through our intuition and emotional landscape as well as *conceptualise the world* and make meaning of it through the logical, rational part of our brain. One part of us is very primal, and the other part is more intellectual. For the most part, I see our intuition and emotional awareness as our authentic nature, and the stories we tell ourselves as our ego mind. Both are designed to help us survive. It's just that our thinking mind sometimes becomes fixated on narratives or perceptions that are essentially untrue (aka limiting beliefs).

So for the first years of life we operate more from the "felt sense", and after three years old, we begin the meaning-making process of our lives. From three onward, we want to understand why things are the way they are, and if we don't know or understand, then our brain will make something up for it to make sense.

A child between the ages of three and eight years old does not have the objective awareness and understanding of human behaviour. They don't know why their caregivers are possibly struggling, how money makes them stressed, why their father is an alcoholic, why their mother has to work four jobs, or why their home is chaotic. All they see is the emotional response from their caregivers. They witness their parents' anxiety, anger, ignorance, unpredictability, or simply their lack of attention when it's most needed. Because of their lack of understanding, children usually conclude that it must be because of *them* in some way. A child's world feels very small, and their needs are a huge part of that small world. If a caregiver is not attuned to them for whatever reason, the simplest way a child can make sense of that is that there must be something wrong with them.

As you can imagine, the meaning we attach to these moments then become our innate core beliefs, which we carry with us throughout our lives. Because they are some of our very *first* beliefs in this world, they feel *very* big and *very* real. Through repetition of these beliefs across the span of our childhood, our brains become wired to see that belief as the truth. And our behaviour adjusts accordingly. We shut down or suppress our authenticity in accordance with those beliefs. We learn how to favour our attachments and ability to survive over our authentic nature and, therefore, our perception of our authentic nature is that it mustn't be good enough.

Takeaway message: Our experiences initiate an emotion, that emotion initiates a belief, that belief drives a behaviour. If the experience, emotion, and belief are repeated consistently, the behaviour turns into a habit.

Journal Questions

* In five words, how would I describe my childhood?
* What are the top three early memories that come to mind instinctively?
* What do I feel were positive attributes of my childhood?
* What do I feel were negative attributes of my childhood?
* What do I know about my birth story, if anything?

The purpose of these five questions is simply to broaden your awareness of your unique childhood experiences. As you reflect on your answers in relation to your current behaviours and thoughts, you may already start to notice some common themes and very valid reasons as to why you do the things you do, or why you think the way you think.

Remember that when exploring childhood experiences, it's important to do so as objectively as possible. This means trying your best not to relive the experiences but rather using your logical brain to seek the data that will help you better understand how it affected who you are today. If answering these questions feels activating or triggering for you, I recommend that you leave them for now and consider exploring them when you are in the safety of someone you trust, such as a trauma-informed coach or therapist.

Lesson 2

Trauma and Toxic Stress

Trauma is a word that is becoming more mainstream as people's awareness of it expands, and we cannot talk about the beliefs that limit and skew our authentic self-expression without talking about trauma. The Merriam Webster dictionary states that the term derives from the Greek word for "wound". So, trauma is a wound. Once upon a time, trauma may have been referred to more in the context of an injury, but nowadays it is not only defined as the physical impact or wounding from an event but also the *emotional* wound that lingers well after an event is over.

One of my favourite definitions comes from physician and trauma expert Dr. Gabor Maté, who I had the pleasure of studying with, learning his unique Compassionate Inquiry—a somatic psychotherapeutic approach to working with people who have suffered from trauma. He states that:

"Trauma is not what happens *to* you, but what happens *inside of you* as a result of what happens to you."

Take a moment to read that a few times. Understanding this statement helps us bring greater awareness as to why some people's experiences of events are indeed traumatic, yet for others those same experiences are not. Ultimately, it's the *meaning* we attach to events and the support—or lack thereof—that we received as they happened. Professor of Psychiatry Dr. Daniel Siegel explains trauma as an event or situation that alters a person's nervous system state, and their beliefs about themselves, others, or the world in a way that compromises their well-being long after the event.

Another way of looking at trauma is through the Buddhist analogy of the two arrows. The analogy states that any time we suffer misfortune, two arrows are flown in our direction. The Buddha explains that we can't always control the first arrow, representing the actual event or situation at hand, but we can control the second arrow if we wish to, representing our response to the first arrow. Being struck by one arrow is bad enough, but being struck by two is much more painful. Trauma is the nonphysical lingering effects of the second arrow, the internal suffering we feel and the story we tell ourselves about being hit in the first place.

There are many different events or situations that can become traumatic for a person, for example, relational trauma, natural disasters, severe illness or injury, sexual assault, witnessing violence, or living in poverty. Trauma can stem from a one-off event, which we refer to as *acute trauma,* or it can develop from an ongoing repetitive experience of the same event, which we refer to as *chronic trauma.* Chronic (ongoing) trauma that happens to a person via several different means is what we refer to as *complex trauma.* For the rest of this chapter, we will be focusing mainly on inter-relational trauma and the underlying stress it creates: the chronic or complex experiences a person may have experienced in relation to their caregivers during their childhood years. The reason we focus on this is because so much of our "not good enough" narratives are born during these formative years. They develop in relation to the child's interpretation of their attachment to their caregivers and their subsequent feelings of safety.

When I first mention childhood trauma to my clients, most of them say to me, "Oh, my childhood wasn't traumatic," or "I haven't experienced trauma like other people have." It's so common to downplay our experiences of trauma because our association with the word is that something *really bad* must have happened (e.g., death, accident, or abuse) for something to be classified as traumatic. And please don't get me wrong, these "big T" events *are most definitely* traumatic. But there are also more subtle events and interactions that can have just as significant an impact on our sense of self, depending on what happened, who was there to support us, and, once again, the *meaning* we attach to them. The number of times a client has told me that, for example, they were hit by their parents when they were "naughty" followed by a shrug of their shoulders and something along the lines of "yeah but that's normal, everyone hits their kids." Is it normal? And even if it *was* normal, does that make it OK? Or is it just a way for the parent to channel their frustration and finally get the obedience they've been wanting? Could there have been an alternative disciplinary choice that did not result in physical abuse? Not only do many of us not acknowledge the trauma that occurred in our lives, but many of us even feel guilty for speaking it out loud. We know that for the most part, our parents tried their hardest with what they knew at the time, and we don't want to go around bad mouthing or being ungrateful. It's good to remember that acknowledging what happened to you doesn't make you ungrateful, nor does it mean you have bad parents. It just means you can see the full picture of your life and start finally making sense of why you feel the way you do. It's perfectly normal for a person to have a great childhood and *also* be impacted by moments throughout that childhood that left a significant impact on their sense of worthiness as an adult.

Dr Gabor Maté explained how trauma is not only the bad things that happen to us but can also be the lack of the good things that should have been there.

Let's read that again: **Trauma is not only the bad things that happen to us but can also be *the lack of the good things that should have been there.***

So, this means that if there was an absence in your early years of required basic needs, such as the need for safety, the need for reliability, the need for human touch/connection, or the need for emotional attunement, then it becomes understandable that the confusion, desperation, and pain experienced by you could result in a belief that leaves you traumatised in some way. A missing factor I encounter a lot with my clients is when there is the absence of support or repair after something difficult happens. I often ask my clients who was there for them at the time or how was that rupture within the relationship repaired after the fact. If the answer is "no one" or "it wasn't" then the impact of the trauma can be more significant because the person is left to deal with their big emotions on their own. Being alone with our hurt (especially as children who don't know yet how to self-soothe or regulate our nervous system) can leave us with a memory of pain that we carry well into our adult lives. And this could be no fault of our parents; perhaps they were just busy people or not very emotionally attuned themselves.

Take Melanie as an example. Melanie was a client of mine who came to me struggling with a really loud inner critic and feelings of complete burnout. No matter what she did or what she achieved, it was never good enough. She could always do better, be better, achieve more. In fact, she thought that everyone around her could also be better, struggling to trust anyone with any task in the fear that they'd get it wrong. She was plagued with an ongoing feeling of emptiness regardless of her accomplishments, and even if she tried to celebrate herself, it fell on deaf ears. From an outsider's perspective, Melanie was very accomplished in terms of how most of society would define the word. She was a surgeon, married to a surgeon, and holding a senior position in an esteemed hospital. She earned a high income, had a dog, a beautiful home in a sought-after suburb, and was trying for her first child. She shared with me that she has an older brother (also a doctor), and a younger sister (a lawyer)—hello, high achievers! They all shared similar qualities of hyper-independence, self-criticism, and a lack of trust in others.

When Melanie and I first started exploring why she felt the way she did, I got curious about what her upbringing was like. As the first conversation opened about her childhood, she said to me "Oh, there's not much there to talk about really". And honestly, that was all I needed to hear.

> **Trauma is not only the bad things that happen to us but can also be the lack of the good things that should have been there.**

As a therapist, I know that usually when a client says something like that to me, it often results in them sharing how their parents didn't really play an active emotional role in their lives. In other words, they did their "job" of ensuring Melanie's basic needs were met: she lived in a big house in a good area, went to a good school, and her family had enough money to live an above-average lifestyle of comfort. They went on an overseas holiday once a year and visited their grandparents every few months. Melanie was involved in extracurricular activities, was great at sport, and graduated her senior year as a valedictorian.

Sounds perfect, right? So, what was missing? After a little more exploration, Melanie shared that her parents (both busy medical professionals), were either physically or emotionally absent from as early as she can remember. She described her mother as never seeming truly interested in her children's lives, and how she never attended any of Melanie's sporting competitions, despite making countless promises that she would. Melanie said her father was "very busy" and often distracted, also giving false promises of more quality time or trips away that never eventuated. He was unemotional and not someone she remembers being physically or emotionally close with. Her family did not talk about emotions, nor did they say "I love you". Physical affection was absent entirely. The only times she felt some sort of connection with her parents was when she achieved high grades or won school trophies. Understandably, that's where she focused her attention.

Melanie's story is a great example of Dr Maté's explanation of trauma sometimes being the absence of the good things that should have been there. The hugs, the positive reinforcement even when she didn't "succeed", the quality time with a loving, present parent asking how she is and how her day was... Now you might be thinking that her childhood experiences were fine, and sure, they were certainly better than many people out there. There was no abuse, no acute traumatic incident, no poverty or serious illness. And yet her internal world felt so crippling. Remember that trauma is ultimately the meaning that we make out of our lived experiences, not the experiences themselves in isolation. So, what then becomes the meaning or the belief of the child when the emotional and physical presence of their caregivers is missing? In Melanie's case, her subconscious beliefs included:

"I am alone."

"I must figure it out by myself."

"I am not a priority."

"I cannot trust that people will do as they say."

"In order to be loved and seen, I must do more."

These beliefs have driven her behaviour. They have played a huge role in her ability for high achievement and "success", and paradoxically, they have also been the catalyst for her burnout, emptiness, self-criticism and self-hatred, as well as her inability to slow down or accept herself as she is.

Another client who comes to mind as I write this chapter is Peter. Peter came to me because he experienced extreme anxiety within his romantic relationships. In fact, his anxiety would be so crippling that he found himself criticising and attacking his partners, saying and doing things he didn't mean to do and always regretted afterwards. These behaviours often caused his relationships to come to an abrupt end. He desperately wanted to understand this pattern of his so that he could show up in relationships as the man he truly knew he was. Peter's childhood situation was different to Melanie's. He grew up an only child, without a father and with a mentally unstable mother who he remembers not seeing for days on end because she would lock herself in her bedroom during her bouts of depression. When she wasn't in her moments of darkness, he remembers constantly walking on eggshells around her, not knowing when she would explode with rage, which often resulted in her throwing things around the house (and at him). He remembers being sent to sit by himself every time he felt emotional or sad, leaving him to face his own confusion and big emotions on his own. Over time he learned how to shut down his emotions, to essentially close off his heart. His various attempts to become close to his mother had unpredictable outcomes, most of which were hurtful to him. Now, as an adult, every time a partner did or said something that he could not predict or control, he felt his anxiety rise in his chest. This was his memory of fear of what would happen next. And his behaviour would become hostile and cold to push away or protect himself from harm. Once he became aware of this connection, he understood that within him still lived that wounded young boy who longed for a consistent, stable parent.

Usually when people have these types of realisations about their internal beliefs, they can initially feel quite angry toward their parents or caregivers. Melanie and Peter both certainly felt this way. This is a normal reaction and totally understandable. Although the expression of healthy anger is an important part of the healing process when it comes to childhood wounds, I don't believe it's helpful to go around blaming our parents for how it all played out. Pointing the finger at them in anger only points the finger away from ourselves and, therefore, our opportunity to change.

It's important here to know two things. First, we can only show up for our children with the understanding and self-awareness that we possess at the time. I don't believe that Melanie's parents were intentionally trying to cause her pain or suffering, but perhaps they were raised in not too dissimilar ways. They weren't emotionally aware themselves, they were high achievers too, and they quite possibly shared the same internal beliefs as she did. That would naturally ripple outward into the way they parent and their own ability to provide emotional attunement. Second, especially in cases like Peter's where abuse or neglect is present, we need to remember that, unfortunately, hurt people hurt, meaning that when we hold on to wounds from our own past that have caused us pain and suffering and that have not been resolved, we tend to project those wounds onto others in ways we probably don't actually want to. Many people simply act from their hurt, without the awareness of why they are hurting, and because they are in pain themselves, the chain reaction is to cause pain around them. Unless the trauma or the pain is relieved, people will continue hurting and will subsequently continue hurting others. This is what we call intergenerational trauma, which we will explore a bit more later.

Mindful Check-In

Talking about trauma can feel exhausting and overwhelming for some. So, let's take a little pause here just to check in on how you're doing. The following exercise is what we call a cyclical sighing breathwork practice. It's a calming breathing exercise recently studied by the Stanford Medical University to help people experiencing heightened levels of stress or anxiety.

* Get in a comfortable seated position, with a tall spine.
* Relax your shoulders, your arms, your face, your jaw.
* Take a normal breath in and out to prepare your body.
* Take an inhale through the nose (fill your lungs about halfway) and hold the breath for 2 seconds.
* Take another inhale through the nose, filling up the lungs completely.
* Now breathe out through the mouth as if you are taking a big sigh. Breathe out for as long as possible until all the air has left your lungs.
* Repeat for 5 to 10 rounds, returning the breath to normal once you're done.
* Check in with how you feel and continue reading.

How trauma shows up in a person will differ greatly depending on the type of trauma, the duration, the age of the person at the time of the event/s, and other surrounding factors including their previous life experiences and norms, their financial situation, who was there to support them, their socioeconomic status, and even a person's race, religion, or gender. For some, it may be easy to identify trauma symptoms when they know they had an explicitly traumatic upbringing; others may find it more difficult to connect the dots. The feelings of shame or anxiety or emptiness are there, and yet their childhood was "good enough". Dr Daniel Siegel, Clinical Professor of Psychiatry at UCLA, identifies trauma as something that shifts our beliefs of how the world "should be" so much that it shocks our system, leaving us in a state of either hyper- or hypo-arousal.

I would identify a person who has unresolved trauma as someone who has become disconnected from themselves and the world around them. This disconnection can show up as anything from anxiety and people pleasing, through to numbness, dissociation, ignorance, busyness, rage, or perfectionism. All these symptoms are just coping mechanisms that humans turn to when they feel disconnected. I use the word *disconnection* because ultimately that's what I think trauma does. It makes us question ourselves and others. We become sceptical about where we belong and who will love us. We can become untrusting. Confused. Defensive even, as if the whole world is out to get us. At the core of all humans is the desire for connection and unconditional love and acceptance. We are born this way. And so, understandably, when we feel our worthiness for this need is questioned, we spend our lifetime trying to conceal our wounds and show up in the world as whoever we think we are supposed to be in order to finally be deserving of the connection we desire. I feel as though so many of us are actually heartbroken without realising it...

In *The Nature of Grief*, John Archer explores the evolution of the emotion of grief. Although most of us may associate grief as something we need to get over, or something that only occurs during moments of death or loss, Archer normalises the emotion as a common human experience that we encounter throughout our lives in many different shapes and forms. In the context of the trauma I speak of, grief is something that can show up many times during childhood when those needed moments of connection and attunement are missing. He writes: "As anyone who ever had separation anxiety as a kid, or who lost track of their parents at the beach, knows, our bodies produce stress hormones when we're separated from our parents, and the only way for these bad feelings to go away is to come together again. This biological reaction to separation keeps us together because staying together provides an evolutionary benefit. Grief, in its most basic form, represents an alarm reaction set off by a deficit signal in the behavioural system underlying attachment."

Along with the emotional and mental repercussions of trauma, we also have physical symptoms. Think of recurring migraines, tension in our shoulders that never seems to go away, ongoing digestive issues, fertility issues, autoimmune conditions, bodily inflammation... All these physical symptoms show us the physical manifestation of toxic stress. Stress, albeit a needed mechanism for survival, can get "stuck" in the body when it is not properly soothed or released. Basically, unresolved trauma shows up as an accumulation of stress. And this accumulation has a wear and tear effect on many of our body systems. Over time, just like the mind, the body becomes exhausted, tense, constricted, and fails to function in a healthy way. The rise in popularity of somatic therapy (*soma* meaning body) helps remedy these symptoms through aiding a person to find a sense of release, safety, and empowerment within their body.

Dr Peter Levine is the founder of a style of somatic therapy called Somatic Experiencing, and in his book *Waking the Tiger* he shares awareness and understanding around the somatic symptoms of trauma. In it he writes:

"The bodies of traumatized people portray "snapshots" of their unsuccessful attempts to defend themselves in the face of threat or injury. Trauma is a highly activated incomplete biological response to threat, frozen in time. For example, when we prepare to fight or flee, muscles throughout our entire body are tensed in specific patterns of high energy readiness. When we are unable to complete the appropriate actions, we fail to discharge the tremendous energy generated by our survival preparations. This energy becomes fixed in specific patterns of neuromuscular readiness. The person then stays in a state of acute and then chronic arousal and dysfunction in the central nervous system. Traumatized people are not suffering from a disease in the normal sense of the word—they have become stuck in an aroused state. It is difficult if not impossible to function normally under these circumstances."

What's important to be aware of as you read this excerpt from his book is that when he uses words such as *threat, injury, fear,* and *survival,* these can be physical *or* emotional. In fact, it can even be *perceived.* The nervous system responds in the same way, whether or not the brain identifies the situation as something that is indeed threatening to our survival. This is why developmental trauma in relation to attachment is so prevalent: As children, our very survival depends solely on the healthy attachment to our caregivers. Any form of threat to this attachment, be it physical or a feeling of not being worthy enough, becomes a felt threat that results in nervous system activation.

One way to tell whether you might have unresolved trauma is through the presence of "triggers" in your life. Do you have unusually strong reactions to certain situations? Like the word *trauma*, *trigger* is a word that gets thrown around a lot, especially on social media. So, for the sake of awareness, let's define what a trigger means in the context of this book. A psychological trigger is when a person has an unusually strong reaction to a stimulus due to the activation of an implicit or explicit memory from their past.

Trigger = a memory from the past resurfacing in present-day situations

So, if trauma happened to us— something that challenged our world beliefs, that threatened our sense of survival in some way *and* something that was not resolved at the time—it's highly likely that we will re-experience these feelings time and time again in everyday situations that remind us in some way of the original event. Like the analogy Dr Maté uses in his teachings, a trigger is not dissimilar to the trigger of a gun: The trigger itself is just a small part of the vessel, which when pushed will cause a big reaction (caused by the ammunition). This reaction, when placed in the context of humans, is usually an emotion or behaviour that we learned at the time of the original experience and that has become imprinted into our system. It comes to the surface during these trigger moments and either causes us to feel shocked or confused at our own behaviour and/or causes others to feel the same way.

Someone who was often given the silent treatment as a child might feel triggered when a person they care about leaves them on read during a text message conversation, which brings up the same feelings of panic that they once experienced as a child. Another example would be a person who felt emotionally or physically abandoned by one of their caregivers. Whenever they have a disagreement with their current partner they may jump to the conclusion that that person is going to leave them, pre-empting an outcome they were familiar with during their first experiences of attachment.

Let's go back to Peter for a moment. Whenever his partner acted in unpredictable ways, it created a chain reaction within him driven by fear for his safety. The anxiety he felt caused his defensive behaviour and his subsequent shutting down and emotional avoidance of that person. The unpredictable behaviour was the trigger of the memory of repeated events with his mother whose unpredictability not only threated his attachment to her (and therefore his survival) but often resulted in chaos and pain of some form. Peter had *no idea* that these adult reactions stemmed from childhood experiences. However, once he was able to properly articulate how he felt in his body and the story he told himself when he was in those triggered moments, he found that they were identical to when he was a child. Simply being aware of this link provided him with an incredible amount of relief. He realised that he was acting in response to a *memory* and not the present moment. This meant that with mindfulness, deeper understanding, and self-acceptance, he had the opportunity to change his behaviours and therefore the quality of his relationships.

When we aren't aware of our triggers, or of our unresolved trauma or subconscious beliefs due to that trauma, we go around living our lives on autopilot. It's not until we can shine a light on what's happening that we can step away from the internal narrative of *What's wrong with me?!* to *What can I learn from this about myself?*

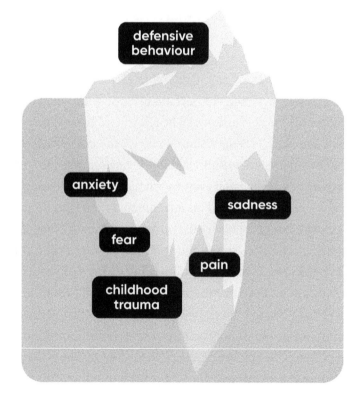

Journal Questions

* Am I aware of any traumatic experiences that occurred in my life? If so, what happened?
* When have I experienced feelings of unsafety, neglect/abandonment, or abuse?
* Do I feel safe in my body in my everyday life? If not, what do I feel?
* Am I aware of what triggers me?
* What parts of me or my past am I scared to uncover, and why?

These questions are designed to build your self-awareness, exploring the difficult and sometimes painful topic of trauma and toxic stress. If any of the questions make you feel uneasy (or triggered), know that you always have a choice and can choose not to answer any that make you feel uncomfortable. Alternatively, you could go through these questions in the safe space of your own therapeutic relationship with your therapist or coach.

Exercise

EXPLORING YOUR TRIGGERS

Triggers offer a profound glimpse into the aspects of yourself that may still carry wounds or need a little extra care and understanding. Feel free to use the following table as you start to explore your recent trigger reactions. By doing so, you are starting to cultivate the skill of compassionate curiosity toward yourself, developing the ability to be a kind and understanding observer. It's in this empathic self-witnessing that you bear witness to the possibilities of healing that lie before you.

What happened	How I reacted	The sensations I felt in my body	The core emotions present	The story I was telling myself	What did these sensations, emotions & story remind me of?	How I would like to have reacted had I not been triggered
My partner got home from work in a bad mood because the traffic was bad.	I felt responsible for his mood and followed him around the house asking if he needed anything. When he wanted to be on his own, I took it personally and felt upset. I apologised when I didn't have to.	A sinking feeling in my stomach. A tension in my shoulders. My heart racing.	Guilt	He's in a bad mood because I have done something wrong. His moods are my responsibility.	Feeling scared and guilty that I had done something wrong as a child and fearing my father's reaction.	I would have liked to have acknowledged and validated his mood but then gone on with my day without allowing it to affect me.

Lesson 3

The Beliefs That Limit Us

All right, now that we have some awareness of what we mean by trauma, and perhaps some awareness of how it shows up through our nervous system reactions and triggers, let's look at how it then correlates to our belief systems. This is a big topic as it basically forms the foundation of this book and explains the question that so many of us ponder on: "Why am I not good enough?"

By gently turning our attention and awareness to our own belief systems, we can further cultivate this skill of self-witnessing. It involves recognising which beliefs may limit you and pull you away from who you authentically are, and which beliefs help you, guiding you toward the version of yourself you wish to be. Your belief systems are like an internal blueprint of how you live your life. They form the "lens" you wear and the perspective you have on yourself, others, and the world at large. They are closely intertwined with your emotions, and ultimately, your core beliefs dictate much of how you experience your life in the present moment. Identifying a person's core beliefs is one of the very first exercises I do with all my therapy clients because it gives us both incredible insight into their subconscious minds.

Your core beliefs are not what you *think* to be true based on what "should" be your beliefs. They are what you intrinsically and instinctively *feel to be true*. There is a big difference between what we know to be logically correct versus how we feel. And oftentimes, the two don't align. "I know that I am worthy of love and kindness, but I don't *feel* like I am." "I know that he isn't going to leave me, but I *feel* like he will." "I know in my head that I shouldn't let her treat me this way, but I *feel* like I deserve it." "I know that my body is fine the way it is, but I always *feel* like I look disgusting." See what I mean?

Dr Siegel's definition of trauma states that when trauma occurs, it is usually an event that challenges our beliefs of how the world should be so much that it shocks our nervous system. For example, a child who desires to be connected to their caregivers but who is instead neglected will most likely develop an internal core belief that they are unlovable in some way. This isn't necessarily a conscious, explicit thought or memory for that person, but rather a deep internal feeling that governs the way they show up in life and relationships. People often aren't even aware that these deep core beliefs exist until we shine a light on them.

Many of the core beliefs that develop in childhood are stored in what we call implicit memory, which we touched on in Lesson 1. This is associated with the right part of the brain that is sensory and feeling-based. The implicit memory is usually what is activated when we are triggered or when we hold perceptions about ourselves that logically don't make sense. The memories stored here are not of logical, conscious awareness and are predominantly feeling-based. There is no time or date stamp to the memory as you would have with an explicit memory, which makes it a lot harder to pinpoint where the feeling is coming from. Nonetheless, it still has a profound effect on us. Our implicit memories are sort of like a constant undercurrent of emotion, shaping our responses and influencing our sense of self in ways we may not always recognise. As we become more attuned to our implicit memories, we gain a deeper understanding of the layers that shape our perception.

For example, I had a difficult and emotionally abusive upbringing with my father. Although he and I are close now and I love him dearly, as a child I was incredibly scared of him. My nervous system was in a constant state of panic and fear whenever I was around him, and his love was very confusing to me. If I did what he wanted me to do, I was loved. If I didn't, I was yelled at, bullied, and punished. What's worse is that I never knew what was right or wrong. It just depended on his mood each day. Understandably, as I grew up my belief about love became that love is scary and conditional. I learned very quickly how to please and appease to avoid conflict and how to keep my emotions to myself. As an adult, my actions within romantic relationships mimicked the same: always that of a people-pleaser. I always said sorry when I didn't have to; I always put my partners' needs before my own. I felt deeply responsible for their emotions and would pander to them in any way I could. I often sacrificed my own happiness, values, or pleasure for the sake of their affection or attention. I tolerated a lot of emotional abuse and disloyalty from my previous partners making up that somehow it was my fault, that I was the one in the wrong, which made them do such horrible things. I'd like to *think* that love is unconditional and equal and fair, but I'd be lying if I said that was how I truly *felt*. At the time of these relationships, I had *no idea* that my behaviours, beliefs, and the patterns I kept falling into were all being guided by my implicit memories. I didn't have the awareness back then that I do now. It took me about eight years of working on and off with a therapist, tending to my inner child, practicing yoga and somatic healing, learning how to confidently communicate and set boundaries, and becoming self-aware for me to change this core belief and show myself a new way forward.

> Our implicit memories
> are like a constant
> undercurrent of emotion,
> shaping our responses
> and influencing our sense
> of self in ways we may not
> always recognise.

Exercise

CORE BELIEFS

Some of your core beliefs will be helpful and relevant to who you are now as an adult, whereas others will be unhelpful and no longer relevant. In fact, they may even be the reason why you don't speak up, or fail to set boundaries, or have people-pleasing tendencies, or always gravitate toward toxic relationship dynamics.

When I first started going to therapy, I held so many beliefs that did not serve me and that contributed to my inner frustrations as an adult. These beliefs had been with me since childhood. One that comes to mind was the belief that other people's emotions are my responsibility. This went hand in hand with the belief that I am guilty. Guilty about what, you might ask. Everything! I just believed that I was always wrong, always guilty, and that everything was my fault. Cue all my people-pleasing tendencies.

After a while, and with a lot of work around actively setting and thinking new, more helpful beliefs, along with taking aligned action toward those new beliefs, the intensity of my old way of thinking lessened as I formed and strengthened new neural pathways in my brain. I learned how to set boundaries without feeling guilty. I learned how to detach myself from other people's emotions and became able to practice empathy without feeling guilty. I learned how to express my needs without the fear of being wrong. This was game changing for me and completely shifted the way I experienced my relationships.

So here's a little exercise on your own core beliefs. You will find a list of words that represent different categories of your life. Your task is to read each word and next to it write down any and all immediate beliefs that come to you. Remember to be brutally honest with yourself. Once you've completed the exercise you will be able to identify quite quickly the core beliefs that are responsible for some of the behaviours or feelings you have, which perhaps you haven't been able to explain up until now. If for any reason you find this exercise too overwhelming or difficult, don't be hard on yourself. It's a great exercise to work on with your own coach or therapist or as a slow self-reflection task that you can work through over time.

CATEGORY	MY CORE BELIEFS
Love	E.g., Love is conditional
Friendship	
Family	
Romantic Relationships	
My body	E.g., I should be thin in order to be attractive
My worthiness	
Success	
Money	E.g., There is never enough
Sex & Intimacy	
Spirituality	

Career	E.g., I must sacrifice in order to succeed
Education	
Health	
Communication	
Emotions	E.g., Being too emotional is embarrassing and weak

So, how and when do our core beliefs form? The Buddha famously said, "With our thoughts, we create the world." Although this is true, it is the world that first creates our thoughts. All children are born with temperament, but it's the environment and the way in which they are nurtured that determines how that temperament develops into what we call personality. What we observe, experience, learn, and hear as children is what offers us the first glimpse of what meaning we attach to the world around us. How we perceive love depends on how we experience it. What we believe about our worthiness depends on the meaning we attached to how we were cared for. The way we respond to conflict depends on how conflict was navigated in our formative years.

When we are born, we are arguably a blank slate. We have a temperament, but we don't know yet what we believe in or value. Our brain develops rapidly as we grow and learn and observe what's happening around us. It's through these observations and experiences that the foundation of our belief systems is formed. We are meaning-making machines, and we are this way because without meaning, the world becomes scary and confusing. Our brain always wants some understanding as to why something is the way it is. We want to feel some kind of sense of safety.

Too many people disregard their childhood experiences because they were "just kids". And as I mentioned earlier in the book, they might belittle or dismiss certain memories, not realising that it's these very memories that still affect who they are today.

The reason I wrote this book is because I have yet to meet someone who doesn't have some aspect of "I'm not enough" etched into their core beliefs. It may sound different for each of us, but the fundamental not enoughness is there.

"I'm not pretty enough."
"I'm not thin enough."
"I'm not successful enough."
"I'm not loveable enough."
"I'm not smart enough."
"I'm not fun enough."
"I'm not interesting enough."
"I'm not worthy."
"I'm not good enough."

Even clients I meet who have the narrative of "I'm too much" are still technically saying they are not enough because they think they are too much.

The problem with feeling like we aren't good enough is that it becomes a breeding ground for shame. And shame is a dangerous and difficult emotion to navigate. We will talk about shame in detail in the next section.

So why do we all go around thinking we aren't enough? That we should be better in some aspect? Why does it always come back to our worth and how we are inherently faulty?

Well, the good news is that you aren't faulty. Not at all. But as a young child, up until the age of seven or so, you *were* egocentric. You were self-centred and thought primarily of yourself, with very little ability to be empathetic of others' emotions or perspectives. This isn't a dig at you. We are all like that as children because it's how we initially learn about ourselves and the world. Swiss psychologist Dr. Jean Piaget was the first person to present a systematic study on how children understand themselves and their environment. His theory suggests that as children we move through four specific stages of cognitive development. This egocentric state is what he coined as The Preoperational Stage (ages two to seven). It's a stage of development when a child is learning language and symbols, as well as expanding their imagination and interaction with others, but is still limited regarding objectivity, empathy, and the ability to see things from an alternate perspective. Take a moment to consider the following: How is a three-year-old expected to understand the world when they are still mastering the art of stringing coherent sentences together? It's just not possible for children to make rational sense as to why their mom is never home, or why their dad has a drinking problem, or why their sadness is always met with punishment.

A child's mind is focused on the very small but hugely important *immediate* world around them... and their focus is on having their needs met. They need to survive, remember? We are still animals, after all, and survival is an instinctive part of our make-up. This means naturally that everything that does or does not happen in a child's life will either be perceived as a threat or a confirmation of their attachment to their caregivers (and therefore their chance of survival).

Because attachment is so crucial in these dependent years, Dr. Maté suggests that a child will always favour attachment over authenticity. This means that they will quickly learn to either suppress parts of themselves *or* develop new behaviours when their authentic nature is not attuned to or nurtured. Because once again, attachment equals survival. Am I sounding like a broken record yet?

Not only do I witness this abandonment of authenticity in my clients' stories of their childhood memories, but I recognise it in my own life, too. I realise how I changed and adapted who I was as a child because I had no choice. If I wanted to survive, I had to sacrifice the parts of me that seemed to make my father angry.

A child's egocentrism, coupled with their immature brain development and their innate primal nature for survival, usually results in core beliefs that are not necessarily true but that would have made perfect sense to them at the time and helped them make meaning out of a situation.

Here are a few examples of what a child's core beliefs could sound like if they were written in coherent language:

"If I am always told to be quiet, it must mean they don't care about what I have to say."

"If I am mocked and belittled, obviously there is something wrong with me."

"If my home is unpredictable and unsafe, that must mean that the world is unpredictable and unsafe."

"If I must take care of myself because no one else does it, obviously I cannot trust anyone."

"I will only be loved if I please them."

"She doesn't yell at me if I am quiet, so I won't speak."

Did any of those beliefs sound familiar to you?

I recently worked with a client who was puzzled about her aggressive reactions during confrontations with her husband, likening it to behaving like a rebellious teenager. Intrigued by this, we delved into the subconscious beliefs guiding her responses. Unravelling the story she told herself during these arguments revealed two core beliefs from her childhood: "I am unlovable" and "I am wrong." In her early years, she strived to please her caregivers, hoping for acknowledgement through quiet compliance or fervent efforts to make them happy, none of which were successful. When her attempts failed, she felt a profound sense of anger and isolation, questioning her own worth. Transitioning into adolescence, her pursuit of connection transformed into a defence mechanism against emotional abandonment, leading to defensive and bitter behaviour. Eventually she was kicked out from home in what she recalls as one of the most heartbreaking moments of her life. It's also the moment that solidified her fears of abandonment. In our sessions, we gently explored the layers of these deep-seated beliefs, recognising the profound impact they had on her emotional responses in her marriage. She came to understand that her reactions were not isolated incidents but rather rooted in her longing for connection and fear of rejection.

As you know by now, many of our childhood beliefs remain with us into adulthood and are what govern many of our decisions. I cannot count the times I have worked with a client who expressed fear around speaking up or communicating, only to find out that their childhood belief was that they were "unheard", "misunderstood", or "wrong".

So, our beliefs dictate our actions and, ultimately, a huge portion of our personality and our reality. Some of our beliefs will be helpful, whereas others will be limiting and unhelpful. Beliefs that are harmful continue to dampen our confidence and self-esteem, leaving us feeling small, hopeless, and depressed or anxious.

Mindful Check-In

You might be acutely aware of some of the limiting beliefs you hold. Even if you aren't aware of them, perhaps after reading this lesson you will have a bit more of an idea of the "monkey mind" that resides within you. The monkey mind is a term you may have heard your yoga teacher use; it's a way of describing what it feels like to have so many thoughts bouncing around in your head like a monkey, a bit chaotic and all over the place. One way of taming the monkey mind is to simply practice noticing the thoughts mindfully, observing which ones aren't true or helpful and compassionately letting them pass by.

You can start practicing this skill by imagining that your thoughts are like leaves on a stream. This meditation practice is adapted from Russ Harris who is the founder of Acceptance and Commitment Therapy (ACT).

1. Find yourself in a comfortable meditation position either sitting up or lying down.
2. Close your eyes or let your gaze soften.
3. Take a few deep, slow breaths to ground your body.
4. Imagine that you are sitting next to a stream of water. It could be a river, a lake, the ocean, or

even a small stream making its way through the forest. Use your imagination and your senses to really set the scene, imagining the sound of the water, the smells, and other things you may notice around you.

5. Try to focus on just watching the stream. It's inevitable that you will have thoughts that distract your attention. When that happens say to yourself *I'm having the thought that...* and imagine placing that thought onto a leaf and letting the stream carry it away. Then, bring your focus back to the stream itself.

6. Continue with this visualisation practice for about 15 minutes, trying to keep your focus on the gentle flow of water, releasing thoughts as they come and watching them float away.

7. After the 15 minutes is over, take a few deep breaths to end the practice and reflect on how you feel.

One aspect of your life where you may really notice the impact of your limiting beliefs is within your relationships, especially your romantic ones. You may have heard of attachment theory. It's a concept coined by British psychologist John Bowlby and later expanded on by psychologist Mary Ainsworth. Bowlby was interested in the emotions an infant experienced in relationship to their caregiver. In particular, the distress or anxiety felt when a caregiver was not attuned to them. What he proposed was that a child requires much more than the basic needs of survival to form healthy learned behaviours in adulthood. They require attunement, responsiveness, availability, and safety, which then creates a sense of inner safety for the child to confidently explore the world around them.

Ainsworth's experiment furthered Bowlby's theory and formed the basis for attachment styles. Her experiment observed the responses of infants between the ages of twelve and eighteen months toward being left and then reunited with their mothers. Depending on multiple factors, the first three attachment styles were created: anxious attachment, avoidant attachment, and secure attachment. Later, in the '80s, the fourth attachment style, disorganised attachment, was added to the list.

Attachment theory helps us connect the dots between our childhood experiences and our beliefs around love and attachment, and how they turn into learned behaviours that we carry with us into adulthood. You might notice that it's usually within romantic relationships where you witness most often the resurfacing of your childhood trauma or unhealed wounds. This is because being in a relationship where we long for acceptance, love, and connection mimics the same desires and needs we had as a child. Although many people I have worked with believe that healing oneself should happen alone, I tend to disagree. I think that it's only within relationships that some of these wounds arise, and therefore it's only within relationships that they have the opportunity to heal. Noticing who you are and how you operate when in love, or even when dating, will give you great insight into the parts of yourself that require nurturance and compassion.

A brief explanation of each attachment style is listed below. You might find this interesting as it can help explain a lot of why we act the way we do within our romantic relationships.

1. Secure Attachment

A person who experiences secure attachment is not preoccupied with worrying if their partner will leave them or whether their partner gets too close to them. They are independent while also being invested in the relationship and do not fear being vulnerable with their significant other. They have a healthy relationship with self and other.

2. Anxious Attachment (and codependency)

A person who experiences anxious attachment is generally very insecure about the relationship and worries often that their partner will leave them. Often associated with feelings of low self-worth, shame, and a desire to people-please, this style of attachment associates independence in the other person as a sign that they are unloved or not good enough.

Codependent behaviour is also common within an anxious attachment style and refers to a dysfunctional relationship dynamic whereby one person's needs are deemed significantly less important than their partner's. The anxious partner will often put their own desires aside for the sake of the other's, will allow their boundaries to be crossed regularly, and will constantly seek the other person's approval or validation in an attempt to avoid conflict or abandonment.

3. Avoidant Attachment
(and hyper-independence)

A person who experiences avoidant attachment has low anxiety scores but experiences a deep inability to trust others. This lack of trust results in an avoidant nature whereby a person would rather have their independence and freedom rather than allow themselves to get close to another person. They need their space and view closeness with scepticism. They assume they will get hurt if they are vulnerable and are more guarded and protective of how they feel.

Hyper-independence is a behaviour we often see within the avoidant attachment style. Along with not being able to trust the other and fearing vulnerability, characteristics of a hyper-independent individual can also include keeping their partner at an arm's distance, being secretive, and feeling unable to ask for help. They are often very focused on their work and tend to be overachievers who are prone to burnout.

4. Disorganised Attachment

A person with a disorganised attachment style experiences both high levels of anxiety and high levels of avoidance. They can be both hyper-independent and codependent, which usually occur interchangeably, making it very confusing for their partners. They are uncomfortable about closeness and vulnerability but also overly concerned that their partner will abandon them. They will move toward and away from their partner and often experience confusion around what they want. This attachment style is the most difficult style to navigate and is often associated with other mental health conditions or issues such as depression, addiction, and suicidal ideation.

Self-Reflection

* ✳ What attachment style do I resonate with the most and why?
* ✳ Where do I notice these behaviours within my current or previous relationships?
* ✳ Where do I feel this comes from when considering my own upbringing?

Exploring your attachment style isn't about making you "wrong" in the way you attach to life partners, but rather about bringing your awareness to the beliefs and behaviours you hold when it comes to something as intimate and vulnerable as love. When we understand our attachment style, we know better how to communicate what we are feeling, what our fears are, and ultimately what we need and where our boundaries lie.

Beyond the meaning we make from our direct interactions with people, we will also make meaning from what we observe. As children we are constantly learning, watching, growing, and figuring out the intricacies of how to do life. It's a bit like the age-old adage: monkey see, monkey do. So, for example, if you observed a mother who was obsessive about her weight and dieting, it's only natural that you might develop a belief that this behaviour is not only normal but that it forms a necessary part of your personal rulebook on how to be human. Similarly, you may have observed a certain type of dynamic between your parents. It's normal to find ourselves repeating the patterns of our parents because it's what we have repetitively seen and learned. A client of mine recently shared with me that she grew up with parents who were always arguing about money and how there was never enough to support the family. As an adult, she, too, felt anxious and worried about her finances, often finding herself picking fights with her husband in the same way her mother would, even though she knew they had more than enough to get by. The unnecessary arguments were causing a strain on the relationship, which she wanted to resolve.

The interesting thing about understanding your beliefs is that so many of them are automatic and subconscious, and they won't even be evident to you until you start observing your actions and asking yourself, *Why am I doing this?* On the subject of beliefs, another facet worth becoming aware of is the concept of intergenerational trauma, briefly introduced in Lesson 1. This phenomenon demonstrates the potential of carrying forward beliefs intertwined with ancestral trauma. Intergenerational trauma was initially recognised in the offspring of Holocaust survivors and has since been studied in various indigenous communities in Australia and North America. This type of trauma encapsulates the unhealed wounds experienced by preceding generations, leaving a legacy of unresolved consequences. The intricate mechanics of intergenerational trauma hinge significantly on the influence of our caregivers. If they bear unresolved trauma stemming from their own lineage, we become witnesses, learners, and unwitting recipients of the pain embedded in their beliefs, behaviours, and actions. Therefore, the cycle persists until someone within the lineage (perhaps even you?) takes the courageous step to disrupt this pattern and initiate the healing journey.

I used to hold a strong core belief that being emotional was bad and that I was bad for expressing my emotions. What I learned throughout my own healing journey and through my awareness of generational trauma is that although my belief was developed for the most part in response to the way my parents raised me, they acted in such ways and held such beliefs because of their own parents, and so on and so on. When I spent the time to dig deeper and understand my cultural lineage, it's not surprising that emotional suppression and denial are traits that run through my roots. For example, just the other day I was speaking to my Italian grandmother about the loss of her husband. He passed away in a mining accident when my mother was just eight years old. My grandmother wasn't allowed to see his body, and the kids—my mother and uncle—weren't to attend the funeral because children were to be kept away from such events. Can you imagine that? Not being able to have the closure of seeing your husband's body? Especially if that is something you wanted, as she did. My grandmother said she never cried in front of my mother in an attempt to "remain strong", hiding her tears behind closed doors when the kids were asleep. She said that this was just how she was taught to be, that being emotional was frowned upon and not to be displayed to the public eye. Women were expected to be private, well put together, and to keep any big emotions under control. I imagined being in my mother's shoes, of not being given the opportunity to properly grieve her dad, not given the opportunity to ask questions as any eight-year-old would want, or to be held by her mother as they wept together and let the tears of shock move through their system as tears are designed to. It's understandable to me that my mother then adopted these beliefs, too, that she would have learned that in order to cope she must hold it all together. She didn't really have much of a choice.

That short snippet into my mom's life is just a tiny, tiny piece of a much bigger puzzle. And that's just *one* side of my family. My father's side had their own aversions and opinions about emotions, and as a result my siblings and I all carry fears of emotional expression to varying degrees. These beliefs that we hold have impacted each of us in unique ways. For me, it's been a lifelong journey to feel safe in vulnerability, to find the confidence to share my emotions, and to not associate emotions such as sadness or fear as inherently bad but rather a very normal and necessary part of a healthy human existence.

When we look at the world at large and the many ingrained beliefs surrounding worthiness, inclusivity, and equality we can see that generational experiences continue to cast long shadows, profoundly impacting millions with histories rooted in slavery, oppression, marginalisation, or segregation. Take, for instance, the era of slavery, when two distinct groups emerged: the enslaved and those who held them captive. Each group, entrenched in their respective roles, developed distinct belief systems. The enslaved, in their struggle for survival, and those who perpetuated slavery. And even though some of these people have the opportunity to rewrite their stories, they will often find themselves living within a society that still has undertones of racism, sexism, and judgement. They may experience daily microaggressions, which can perpetuate a person's trauma despite their attempts to escape it or heal from it. The sad thing is that a lot of people probably don't want to be racist, sexist, or biased, but because they are unconscious to their own belief patterns, their behaviour and attitude will reflect as much. So much of humanity is still completely oblivious to their unconscious beliefs, which is why generational cycles can be hard to break. As Carl Jung famously said, "Until you make the unconscious conscious, it will direct your life and you will call it fate."

If you feel called to explore further, you may wish to consider and source information on your own family history. You may become curious about whether some of your own beliefs and behaviours are due to repeated patterns or coping mechanisms that stem from generations before you.

Journal Questions

* What beliefs do I hold about myself that I know logically are not true but cannot shake the feeling of?
* What parts of myself am I afraid to show to others, and why?
* If money, judgement, shame, and fear did not exist, who would I be, and what would I be doing?
* How much do I actually know about my own family history and the impact that generational experience may have on my current belief systems?

Lesson 4

How The World Shapes Our Beliefs

The final lesson of this step is to understand the impact of society, culture, and media on our belief systems. In the previous chapter, we looked at how our early core beliefs are formed, but what happens once we enter the outside world? How are our beliefs shaped then?

Growing up within a multicultural family, I have had the privilege of experiencing the contrast of beliefs and expectations between religions, languages, customs, traditions, and gender roles. My mother was born a Catholic Italian who grew up in Australia, and my father, a melting pot of Indonesian, Arabic, and German, grew up in an Islamic family living in Indonesia. I was born in Australia and moved to Indonesia in my infancy, where I was homeschooled and later attended a co-ed national school that combined both Indonesian and expatriate teachers and kids. For high school we moved back to Australia where I attended a private, all girls, Anglican school. I feel lucky to have been a child raised with such diversity. My parents were faced with what I can only imagine as a difficult task of merging multiple cultures. We celebrated both Ramadan and

Christmas, spoke both English and Indonesian, attended classes in Italian and Arabic for a certain period, ate gnocchi and nasi goreng, and prayed in churches and mosques. Better yet, we were given—for the most part—the freedom to explore and discover for ourselves which elements of these cultures and religions resonated with us the most. Of course, certain beliefs impacted my own views on who I "should be" to be a successful, worthy woman, but for the most part we had an environment that promoted choice and curiosity. I distinctly remember my grandfather, a devout Muslim, telling me that it doesn't matter which religion I choose and what matters most is that I am a good-hearted person who treats myself and others well. He told me that regardless of what text you read or what religion you follow, it is operating from the heart that is at the essence of it all. I remember thinking that was pretty special. I truly believe that living and witnessing such diversity has given me an open-minded and objective approach to people and life itself, and I am forever grateful to my parents for providing me with such experiences. Now, as a therapist, this objective, broad lens has enabled me to better understand my clients and to easily shift perspectives whenever I need to, in order to see things through their eyes.

I respect that not everybody has had this experience, though, and if we were to take just one aspect of my background in isolation and imagine a person who lived purely through that lens, we could easily see how quickly they would be conditioned to view life in a certain, possibly much more rigid, manner. The gender expectations within Indonesia, for example, are still relatively biased. The men have certain privileges the women do not. Women are still primarily expected to behave a certain way. The country still does not recognise the marriage of two people with separate religions. Homosexuality is still frowned upon by many. There is a distinct class divide between rich and poor. Even the topic of mental health issues was taboo until recent years. When my mother fell pregnant with my older sister, she was told by my father to stop working. The traditional idea that she was a mother and could not have a career has, to this day, left some resentment within her. I would say some of these more traditionalist beliefs have filtered down to us kids as well. The stereotypical masculine/feminine gender roles around money, emotions, career, parenting, dating, and the like were strong beliefs I held for a long time... and still do to an extent.

So, the invitation here is to simply start taking a bird's-eye view of the influences outside of the direct way in which you were cared for. Consider the situations, cultural norms, gender roles, economic situation, and religious influence that you were exposed to (and perhaps still are) to better understand how and why you—or your parents—hold some beliefs.

As we continue to explore how society affects our beliefs, we can revisit the topic of discrimination and segregation and the fact that it is still happening every day, right in front of us. This under-standably makes it difficult for someone who is trying to break free from their limiting beliefs of being "unworthy" or "lesser than" because there is still so much evidence that proves their beliefs to be true. When individuals are subjected to discrimination, they often experience a sense of marginalisation and exclusion through both macro and microaggressions from mainstream society. This will perpetuate their feelings of inadequacy and low self-esteem, which can then limit their potential. For example, someone who still experiences racial discrimination, even though they logically know they are worthy regardless of their race, may come to believe that they are not good enough or that they do not belong due to the way that they are looked at, spoken to, or how assumptions are made about them. This can lead to feelings of shame and self-doubt, which will affect their confidence in all aspects of life.

Discrimination can also create barriers to accessing resources and opportunities, further reinforcing limiting beliefs and shame. For instance, someone who experiences gender discrimination may not be able to pursue the career they desire, which can lead to more feelings of inadequacy and the belief that they are not capable. This can have a lasting impact on their self-worth and can be difficult to overcome.

Breaking free from limiting beliefs and shame requires a willingness to challenge and question these internalised messages, which, once again, will be incredibly hard in a society that still reinforces the very thing they are trying to disprove. The systemic nature of discrimination refers to the way in which discrimination is embedded and perpetuated within social, political, and economic systems and institutions. This means that discrimination is not just a result of individual biases or prejudices but is also perpetuated through the policies, practices, and norms adopted by institutions and organisations.

For example, systemic discrimination can occur in the workplace, where certain groups may face unequal pay or limited opportunities for advancement. It can also occur in the criminal justice system, where individuals from certain racial or ethnic groups are disproportionately incarcerated. These systemic forms of discrimination create a cycle of disadvantage and marginalisation that can be difficult to break and can shape beliefs and experiences for generations.

This is where it becomes so important and so necessary for all humans to understand how we impact one another, to reflect on what type of society we want to cultivate for ourselves and our children, to choose our leaders wisely, and to check in on our own values and ensure that we lead by example.

The above is a very brief snapshot of the sociocultural beliefs that can be present within society and how they then ripple out to affect us as individuals and our internal narrative about who we are or are not. Some beliefs will be useful and helpful to us, and some won't. Perhaps now is an opportune moment for you to consider how your environment affects your own beliefs about self or the world. You can also consider how the way you show up within your society might impact others.

Self-Reflection

* Where do I notice unfair or unconscious segregation or discrimination within my own community or social system?
* How do my own beliefs and biases perpetuate the ongoing battle for equality between humans?
* If I could change one thing about the way I view others or myself, what would it be and why?

When I lived in Australia, I used to give a lot of talks for young women at the different schools around my area. Their ages tended to range from twelve to seventeen years old, and the topics I spoke about most were body image and self-worth. When I was a clinical nutritionist, I worked extensively with women who suffered from disordered eating or eating disorders, so I was interested in speaking to young women, hoping I could help them cultivate awareness around these issues before they became problematic. I was always shocked at just how early some of these self-destructive beliefs were being formed.

Some of these girls' beliefs arose from watching a caregiver obsess about their own weight and/or obsess about the child's weight from a very young age. It's not uncommon for me to work with clients who tell me how they were put on a diet from the age of four, or who were teased about their weight or the way they looked (usually by a family member) from as young as three years old. For others, their sense of unworthiness stemmed from a similar place as my own: having a disconnect from one of their caregivers and the feelings of shame, confusion, and hurt which came with it. Many fell victim to the more obvious culprits, such as the beauty industry and fitness world. These are multibillion-dollar industries that market directly to people's pain points. Their images, slogans, or products are by design intended to activate someone's "not good enoughness" and further enforce the belief that who they are, as they are, is inadequate. They *must* buy those protein shakes. They *must* have cellulite-free thighs. They *must* get the lip filler. They *must* purchase the $500 caviar-infused face cream. If they don't then they just won't be worthy of society's approval. It sounds so harsh, but these are the very basics of marketing. You make someone believe they need something by creating the belief that without it, they will not obtain success or love. And as we all know, one of the primary human needs (outside of food and shelter) is the desire to be connected and attached. One of the greatest human fears is the fear of rejection or abandonment. Market to this pain point, and you should be able to sell just about anything. Once again, the invitation here is to take a bird's-eye view and consider how your exposure to advertising, movies, magazines, billboards, and the beauty or health industry has impacted your personal belief system on who you "should" be. Do you recall ever comparing your teenage body to that of an adult? Or fussing about your food and calorie counting because that's what your mom did? Which messages did you receive about your body or looks growing up? Did you ever develop the belief that aesthetics are more important than authenticity?

Mindful Check-In

Taking in all this information and applying it to our own lives can be exhausting, and we will inevitably be filled with ideas, memories, and questions. With that said, let's take another quick mindful break to reground before we continue.

This exercise helps us activate our parasympathetic nervous system through the oculocardiac reflex, which in simple terms is a reflex that slows down our heart rate when we relax our eyes. So, get comfortable in your chair, and let's do this simple, quick practice.

✳ If you are wearing glasses, take them off.
✳ Rub the palms of your hands together to generate warmth and heat.
✳ Cup your palms and place them over your eyes, gently pressing into your eye sockets (don't push the eyeballs but just press around the eye sockets).
✳ Allow your eyes to rest into the darkness and warmth.
✳ Stay like this for 30 seconds to 1 minute.
✳ Slowly remove your hands from your eyes and check in with your body and nervous system.

Now that we have our sense of grounding back, let's continue our exploration. This time, the influence of social media...and what a fascinating beast that is. I often find myself thankful I didn't have a phone and social media when I was in school. Social media truly can influence us both positively and negatively in such powerful ways. Don't get me wrong, I use social media myself and curate it to suit my values, business, and interests. But many people, especially young teens, don't. They want to follow famous people, beauty bloggers, lifestyle influencers, diet trends, and fill their feeds with images of the "dream life". Although I have seen a shift in social media lately, with more people sharing real stories or images, we still see a highlight feed of a superficial existence delivered through a lens of beauty-enhancing filters or carefully photoshopped representations of what it means to be "perfect". Now, with the explosion of AI, we simply don't know or can't even tell what's real or what isn't. People follow accounts that are completely AI generated, perhaps not even realising that the person they are following does not in fact exist. Depending on what your feed looks like (if you use social media) and what your limiting beliefs are, this space can be a dangerous escape to have at your fingertips. The obsession and addiction to getting more and more followers and more and more "likes" fuels the belief that our worth is dependent on someone else's opinion of what we look like and what we are doing. We develop the unhealthy habit of opening our phones to obtain a quick hit of dopamine instead of finding other activities that inevitably make us feel better for longer. As if this wasn't enough, the different algorithms used within these platforms literally can know you and your interests better than you do, delivering more ads and videos and content of the exact things that are slowly but surely damaging your sense of worthiness.

When I started writing this book, I was about six months pregnant with my first child. And right now, as I make the final edits before publishing, my little boy is 18 months old. As a new mother I have felt so much pressure and used to hold so much judgement, especially in his first few months of life, for some of the choices I did or did not make. As many new parents do, I started to follow different accounts during my pregnancy because I wanted to learn as much as I could about the birthing process, about infant sleep, and development, about how to introduce solids, and ultimately, how to be a "good" parent. Don't have a cesarean. Make sure you delay cord cutting. Ensure adequate skin-to-skin contact. Don't feed your baby formula. Don't give them a bottle. Do give them a bottle. Don't sleep train them. Do sleep train them. Don't co-sleep with them. Do co-sleep with them. Make sure you slice their grapes like this and not like that. On and on the list goes. Now, this isn't a dig at businesses that share insight on the journey of birth or parenthood, but rather an observation of what it feels like when you're reading one thing after another and feeling more and more confused because so much of it is contradictory. If anything, following so many accounts on the topic totally pulled me away from my own intuition and my natural connection to my body and my baby, and so I made the decision (thank goodness) to unfollow all the accounts that made me second-guess myself. Sometimes, even if the content is designed to be helpful, it can make us feel worse. In these moments we must remember to come back to self.

I remember the birth of my son like it was yesterday. He was already 2.5 weeks past his due date, meaning I was over 42 weeks pregnant and feeling very, very big. I started having natural contractions the morning I was scheduled to be induced. They started around 6 a.m. and by 9 a.m. I was having contractions every few minutes. By 10 a.m. it was around every 1.5 minutes. I won't go into the details of what it's like to be in labor, but feeling such intensity throughout my body with little rest time in between is hard work. Six hours later and I was still only two centimetres dilated. Can you imagine? Two centimetres! I had to get to ten...

In that moment I knew that something was not quite right. My intuition told me that my body did not want to open, that it did not want me to dilate. We gave it another hour. Still no change. The contractions were still as intense and still as strong. I remember the doctor saying that the way I was contracting and the frequency was as if I was at least eight or nine centimetres dilated. We placed the heart monitor on my belly to check how the baby was doing. And we all heard and saw on the graph how his heartbeat was dropping significantly with every contraction. I remember in that moment knowing that I had to make a decision to honour my baby, not my ego. I knew I wasn't meant to birth him vaginally, and yet I had tears streaming down my face because I felt like I had already failed. It seems like everyone tells you that a "natural" birth is a vaginal one, and many schools of thought imply that if you cannot have a vaginal birth, then somehow you will be numb to your experience as a mother. I remember my doula looked at me, squeezed my hand, and asked me why I was crying. I told her how I felt bad and wrong that I was deciding to have a cesarean. She replied, "Nikki, there is no right or wrong way to give birth. Birth is birth. Listen to your body." It was exactly what I needed to hear, and in that instant my shame disappeared and I was able to go into the OR with a sense of peace and strength and trust. My baby was delivered quickly and easily, and I got to cuddle him and feed him immediately before he was taken away to be wrapped up. I felt a wave of relief, thinking that I would soon follow him and it would all be over, but instead, I stayed on the operating table a good hour longer than expected...

The doctor peered over the sheet that separated us as I was lying there and asked, "Nikki, is this your first pregnancy or not?" I know he was trying to remain calm and had I not had such extensive experience in reading human emotion I probably wouldn't have picked up on it, but his eyes looked worried and slightly fearful. I could sense something was wrong. I honestly replied no. I have had two abortions—one at 18 and one in my mid-twenties. Both were unpleasant but necessary. His head disappeared back behind the sheet and I was left wondering what was happening. Finally, I was stitched up and wheeled out into recovery where I could be with my baby and family. When he came to see me later that night to check how I was doing, he explained that I had a rare, high-risk condition called placenta accreta, something that affects less than 2 percent of pregnancies. My placenta had attached itself to the scar tissue from my previous abortion and had grown into the muscle and tissue of my uterus. This is not easily detected through ultrasounds or scans so it's not possible that we would have picked up on it earlier. He told me that in many cases, the outcome of this condition (especially if the baby is birthed vaginally) is either the removal of the uterus completely or severe cases of life-threatening bleeding and haemorrhage. I had goosebumps all over my body. I thanked him for helping me and he said, "Don't thank me, thank god." I had known in my body that something was wrong. I knew that I couldn't and should not birth vaginally and yet, everything I had read, everything I had heard, caused a deep shame to wash over me, which kept pulling me away from my inner guidance.

As I write about my experience of becoming a mother, I can't help but think about my client Lauren. She messaged me seeking therapy for postpartum anxiety and depression. Her little one was about four months old when we first started working together, and to put it bluntly, she was a mess. The first few months post

> The obsession and addiction to getting more and more followers and more and more "likes" fuels the belief that our worth is dependent on someone else's opinion of what we look like and what we are doing.

birth are exhausting, confusing, and emotional as it is, but when we add a good dose of shame on top of that, it can send the mind into very dark places. She, like me, had been exposed to the same messages from social media, society, and her doula regarding the "right" way to birth and parent. Unlike me, she had a vaginal birth, but she opted for an epidural. Her baby was suctioned out and on her birth report it stated that "mother was too tired to push". The way she interpreted this was that she had already failed at being a "good" mother. This was the first blow to her heart. Being born with jaundice, her baby was taken away from her to spend a few days in the NICU. Blow number two. When she did eventually have time with her baby, she struggled to feed him due to having inverted nipples. Blow number three. This sequence of events fuelled a narrative within her, convincing her of her inadequacy as a mother. She would often say to me, "I can't do this." She found herself constantly comparing her journey to those portrayed on social media—home births in flower-filled water baths, or mothers effortlessly traveling with their babies. The weight of shame brought forth emotions of anger, anxiety, sadness, and hopelessness. Collaboratively, as we delved into Lauren's experience, it became apparent that her belief of incapability wasn't a new sentiment but a long-held belief rooted in childhood. Raised by a perfectionistic mother who wielded fear for control and love with conditions, Lauren had grown up feeling perpetually inadequate. Together we reworked some of her beliefs, we challenged them, and we found ways to bring more compassion and understanding to her experiences as a mother. With time, Lauren discovered an unexpected reservoir of resilience within herself, realising that every challenge she faced had actually made her more capable than she had ever imagined.

When we revisit our relationship with social media, how much power do our devices truly have over our mental health? I can tell you right now that when I asked that room of girls who had issues with their body, over 80 percent of them raised their hands. When I asked how much of that was due to social media, another 80 percent of that group kept their hands in the air. So, in my opinion, the answer to that question is *a lot.*

If you think about it, there is so much stimulation all around us: video, audio, imagery, reels, photos, TikToks... and that's outside the general advice, opinions, and ideals projected onto us by teachers, friends, colleagues, religious bodies, medical systems, government policy, and cultural expectations. There are *so* many stimuli and so much data to process, all of which have the ability to influence our beliefs, perceptions, and values and either move us further away from, or closer toward our authentic selves.

Journal Questions

✳ Do I feel pressure to live up to certain societal expectations? If so, which ones and where does the pressure come from?

✳ What do I believe will happen to me if I don't achieve the expectations I place on myself from society/culture/religion?

✳ If I didn't feel that I had pressure from the outside world, how would it impact me?

✳ How does social media influence my thoughts and beliefs, either positively or negatively?

✳ What is my relationship like with my body, beauty, and diet, and where did these come from?

Step 2

Understanding

You made it to Step 2! I know that Step 1 was a *big* step with a lot of information to process. The awareness piece is huge, and without awareness we don't get very far in our journey of self-discovery and growth. In fact, I would say that being more aware is most of the work done. Without awareness, we cannot know what needs to be done, we cannot develop the willingness to change. We cannot see the multiple possibilities in front of us. We need to open our eyes and become more conscious to realise exactly where we've come from, what was happening around us, and how these aspects of our lives influence our behaviours today. Becoming aware allows you to view things in a different light. You can understand that there are elements at play much greater than *just you* and that the way you operate now is not because you are bad, wrong, or faulty, but rather because you are a product of your lived experiences and the generational experiences before you.

In this step of understanding, we take our broad awareness and start to narrow it slightly by applying more of our personal story to it. We begin to *understand* the manifestation of our lived experiences into our current reality and see *why* we do the things we do or feel the way we feel.

Lesson 5

Your Critical Voice

How many rules do you have for the way you *should* live your life? How many times do you catch yourself criticising your choices? How often do you get frustrated or angry with yourself for making a very normal, human mistake?

As strange as it may sound, we all have many different voices or "parts" that exist within us. Although not always helpful, these internal voices mean well, endeavouring to safeguard us and foster meaningful connections. In the initial stages of self-discovery and exploration we usually come face to face with our inner critics. This internal voice is often an unforgiving, hyperaware narrator who casts judgement over our every move with relentless precision. Succumbing to its ceaseless commentary can prove utterly draining.

Lauren's post-birth inner critic vividly illustrates the magnitude this internal voice can reach, undermining our capacity to function optimally and eroding our self-trust and compassion. Yet, as with any aspect of our inner landscape, delving into its true purpose often reveals invaluable insights. Within the relentless chatter, we might realise what it is trying to protect us from.

It's normal to hate on our inner critic. To wish it wasn't there. After all, it's not a nice feeling to be scrutinised consistently, is it? But what if I told you that the purpose of the critic was that of good? An inner guardian fiercely dedicated to our safety and connection. It operates with a vigilant eye, scanning for potential threats and navigating the delicate terrain of relationships. Though its delivery may lack finesse, its underlying motive is to shield us from harm and ensure a sense of belonging. The inner critic has remembered every single time you have ever been hurt, experienced pain, been rejected, abandoned, or ridiculed. It remembers feeling alone. It remembers heartbreak. It remembers it all. And understandably, it feels stressed and anxious about all of it. Your critic never wants you to feel these things again, so it actively tries to steer you away from potential danger by telling you how you should or should not be, what you should or should not say, and what you should or should not do. It's almost like an overprotective big sister who shouldn't really be parenting you but has no one else around to help her. She loves you dearly but doesn't have the tools to do it in a nicer, more nurturing way. In fact, this inner critic of yours, as bossy as she may seem, is actually longing for someone else to take the lead. The problem is, she doesn't trust anyone.

Although there are many ways you can get to know your inner critic, one route is to start by exploring your "should" statements. It's a fascinating exercise, and I'm sure you will be surprised at just how many internal rules, regulations, and unrealistic expectations you hold yourself accountable for.

As your childhood unfolded and your understanding of the world deepened, you would have learned behavioural patterns essential for cultivating a sense of safety and, ideally, love. Throughout our lives, we construct a subconscious list detailing the ways we "should" and "should not" be to garner acceptance and feel deserving of these fundamental needs. Your inner critic diligently started recording these nuances from the moment you entered the world! For those with perfectionistic tendencies, the effort required to meet such an extensive list of expectations is undoubtedly familiar, highlighting the taxing nature of maintaining these high standards.

Now you might be thinking, *What on earth are "should" statements, and how do I know what mine are?* All you have to do is get a piece of paper and write down the beliefs about who you think you "need to be" in relation to the following categories. When doing this exercise, however, it's imperative that you focus on your automatic, immediate beliefs, and not the beliefs you *think* are correct. It is similar to the exercise you did in the previous step.

For example, earlier in the book I explained how one of the beliefs I held for a long time was that love is conditional. I know logically that true love is not, nor should ever be, conditional as it goes against the very meaning of the word. But due to my own experiences of receiving love, it's what I believed to be true. Therefore, if I were to explore who I thought I needed to be in order to be loved, my "should" statements would have sounded like these:

"I should put my partner's needs before my own in order to be loved."
"I should aim to please my partner as often as possible."

> "I should ensure that my partner's requests are met."
> "I should not upset my partner."

This is not an exaggeration. This is genuinely how I believed I should act within romantic relationships and even close friendships for most of my life. They are the very rules that kept my people-pleasing tendencies alive, that allowed others to cross my boundaries, and that landed me in many toxic partnerships. These statements were a direct result of my core belief that love is conditional. My learned behaviour as a child was to hide anything that may disappoint my father (even if that meant lying), to be agreeable at all times, to not express myself authentically, to not get upset, and to do whatever he said. If I followed these rules, I would (hopefully) experience a sense of safety and love. If I didn't, I would experience punishment, ridicule, and fear.

As you do this exercise, what you may start to realise is that many of your "should" statements no longer apply to your life. Others may still be very relevant and closely linked to your core values and the person you desire to embody as you grow and develop. You are not a child anymore and do not need to operate as if you were in the same environment that you once were. You have choice and freedom now. You are no longer dependent. You no longer need to prove your worthiness.

A client of mine was doing this exercise with me not too long ago. She grew up in multiple foster homes. Her biological mother was an alcoholic, and her father had mental health issues. She experienced sexual and physical abuse and to survive had to learn very quickly how to be independent. She learned that people cannot be trusted and that if she wanted anything in life, she had to do it on her own. Her "should" statements didn't allow her to be open, vulnerable, compassionate, or calm. The rules she placed on herself were harsh, rigid, restrictive, and understandably ensured that she was protected from everyone and everything by closing herself off to the world. As a result, she pushed away potential loving relationships, self-sabotaged every time she felt like her life was going well, criticised herself constantly, and was incredibly defensive.

> What if I told you that the purpose of the critic was that of good? An inner guardian fiercely dedicated to our safety and connection.

It's completely rational, though, that as a child she would have developed these rules. They were *needed* to keep her safe. After all, what would *any* child think or believe about themselves and the world if they were in the same situation? These rules are not bad or wrong. They were essential to her survival. But as an adult, she realised that they weren't serving her. They prevented her engaging in healthy romantic relationships, they restricted her friendships, she always felt lonely, and her body was consistently in a heightened state of stress. This resulted in physical ailments, ongoing migraines, and inflammation within her cervix. She knew she wanted to change and didn't understand why she couldn't. It wasn't until she commenced therapy and became more aware and understanding of her patterns that she realised just how much her subconscious mind was keeping her stuck—that her internal rules were so strict that her authentic self could not breathe. We worked through her rules, spending time with each one, offering them validation, compassion, and curiosity. She learned what she needed to release the rules that no longer served her and was able to embody and enact new rules and behaviours that were more in alignment with who she longed to be.

So now it's your turn to have a go. Here is a list of categories (in no particular order) for you to write to, along with some real-life examples of "should" statements from my clients. Remember that your "should" statements will be both positive and negative. Some will be of great use to you now, whereas others will not be as useful. I've provided examples of both. Feel free to add more categories to this list if you want to.

Category	Example
Love/Romantic Relationships	I should do as my partner wishes otherwise he/she might leave me. (Not useful) I should be a good listener to my partner and try to not take everything personally. (Useful)
Family	My family should support me financially even as an adult. (Not useful) My family should support my aspirations in life and encourage me during my challenging times. (Useful)
Spirituality	I must adhere to my family's religious beliefs even though I don't believe in them myself. (Not useful) I should respect other people's spiritual practices even if I hold different views. (Useful)
Friendships	I should say yes to doing things I don't want to do otherwise I might not be accepted by my friends. (Not useful) My friends should be supportive of my wishes for alone time and space. (Useful)
Career	I should not make mistakes at work because it means I won't be successful and that I am a failure. (Not useful) I should seek help when I do not know something and be forgiving of my humanness. (Useful)
Beauty/Physical Appearance	I should be skinnier/bigger/taller/shorter/have lips like hers/have a smaller bust.... (Not useful) I should appreciate my body because it is so much more than just aesthetics. (Useful)
Money	I should marry someone with lots of money because I know I'll never be successful on my own. (Not useful) I should strive to learn about financial security so I'm not in a position where I cannot support myself. If someone else can also contribute to that, it's just a bonus. (Useful)

You will have more than just one or two "should" statements per category, so take your time with this and see what comes up. Once you've written everything down, reflect on how this exercise made you feel and whether it has opened your eyes to the rules you place yourself under. A few questions you could ask yourself include: Are the majority of your "should" statements helpful or unhelpful? Were there some you know you developed as a coping mechanism but which don't serve you anymore? What else comes up for you as you reflect on the standards you set for yourself?

When it comes to healing your inner critic, a big part of the journey is in understanding that it serves as a mechanism for protection, not for harm. When you can truly wrap your head around this and offer compassion to yourself for what your critic is trying to do, you can start to respond to it differently, offering more validation, support, encouragement, and tenderness during the moments when it feels afraid. We will explore how to do this later in the book.

Journal Questions

* What are the most common phrases or statements I tell myself that are critical?
* When and why do I think these statements formed?
* How do/did these statements keep me safe?
* What do I think this part of me needs in order to not critique myself or feel afraid any more? (Think about things such as boundaries, risks, words of affirmation, trust, etc.)

Lesson 6

Shame

It would be impossible to talk about our not-good-enoughness without talking about shame, as shame is a core emotion and often sits in the driver's seat.

In my opinion, shame is of the most debilitating emotions. Not much good comes from it, and if we get stuck in it, we can rapidly find ourselves in cycles of self-sabotage, anger, comparison, addiction, self-harm, and depression.

So what is shame, and how do we navigate such a difficult state of being?

I love how Brené Brown describes shame and separates it from the very normal (and not dangerous) emotion of guilt. To put it simply:

Guilt: "I did something bad."
Shame: "I am bad."

If we inherently believe we are bad in any aspect, then we get stuck in a corner. There's no way out, no option for redemption.

Guilt leaves room for forgiveness and understanding of mistakes, whereas shame tells us that we are flawed, broken, and unable to be fixed. In over a decade of working within this field, the root cause for so many symptoms I see—perfectionism, trauma bonds, drug abuse, love addiction, self-harm, disordered eating, obsessive exercising—is shame.

And if you haven't guessed it already, shame starts in childhood. Given the right ecosystem, it will grow and grow and grow until it completely suppresses our true nature.

Here are the perfect conditions in which shame can grow exponentially and get into the driving seat:

1. Negative Confirmation Bias

Confirmation bias is when we give more attention to, and actively seek out evidence to prove a belief to be true, while ignoring or rejecting any evidence that could disprove it. *Negative bias* is the tendency for the brain to focus more on negative events, memories, and thoughts rather than positive experiences. When you combine the two, you get negative confirmation bias. This is the conscious and subconscious seeking of evidence to prove negative beliefs or thoughts to be true.

Research suggests a few different reasons why we do this. The most common explanation is that it's a result of human evolution and natural desire to avoid danger and to fit in to our tribe or community for purposes of survival. It makes sense, right? If I want to stay safe, free from danger, and have a tribe to protect me and my offspring, then it's understandable that I would be assessing every situation for risk and homing in on anything and everything that threatens my existence.

Another explanation is that the brain's receptors for negative stimuli are significantly more reactive than when exposed to positive stimuli. For example, let's say you post a picture on Instagram and receive 100 positive comments and two critical or negative comments. Your brain will focus on the negative, and those two comments will feel way more impactful than the 98 positive ones. Annoying, right? So, when our mind encounters negative experiences, they are more impactful, and therefore the *awareness* toward the possibility of negative stimuli is also heightened. Once again, this is a measure to keep us safe.

For most of us, this bias occurs so automatically we don't realise it's even happening, which can obviously make it harder to become aware of. So, if we feel shameful about an aspect of ourselves, and negative confirmation bias is happening subconsciously and simultaneously, it means we will automatically be finding more and more reasons to justify our shame story. Obviously, the more reasons we find, the stronger the neural connections become and the more "true" it feels. For instance, let's say someone has always struggled with public speaking and feels deeply ashamed about their perceived lack of eloquence (maybe this belief was formed in childhood because they were bullied at school for their slight stutter). In social situations where they have to speak publicly, their negative confirmation bias kicks in automatically. They may subconsciously focus on moments when they stumble over a word or receive less-than-enthusiastic feedback from the audience. As a result, they reinforce their belief that they are inherently bad at public speaking. With each perceived failure, their shame story is validated, strengthening the neural connections associated with their feeling of inadequacy. Over time, this reinforces the belief that they are indeed a poor public speaker, making it even harder to challenge and overcome their insecurities.

2. A Relentless Inner Critic

The human brain, unlike any other animal, has the ability for a hugely expansive creative imagination and a much broader ability for cognitive processing. It's this development and ability of the brain that has allowed our species to evolve the way we have, develop and learn language, decipher complex mathematical problems, hypothesise theories, and express and feel our full emotional landscape.

The imagination can also get us caught up in ideas and thoughts that are dangerous to our self-esteem and sense of worthiness. It is this same functionality that expands potential, which paradoxically also has an ability to create false narratives and stories about ourselves, limiting our potential. As we explored in the previous lesson, our brain can create stories about ourselves or others that feel so true we can't help but manifest them into reality and behave as if they are gospel.

The inner critic is that part of ourselves that judges, criticises, and belittles us. It questions our authenticity and our intuition and keeps us living in a state of fear and restriction. Many people try to silence the inner critic; however, I find that silencing it or ignoring it can actually make it worse. The inner critic, if not understood, can become catastrophic to our self-worth and can quickly become

> In over a decade of working within this field, the root cause for so many symptoms I see—perfectionism, trauma bonds, drug abuse, love addiction, self-harm, disordered eating, obsessive exercising—is shame.

the loudest and most convincing voice in our head.

When the critic is not understood, or when the critic is in the driver's seat, it becomes the voice that perpetuates shame. Like the devil on our shoulder, it's always reminding us of our shame story and how what we are doing or who we are is bad or wrong. The critic is often responsible for behaviours such as reclusion and isolation, defensiveness, avoidance, people-pleasing, self-sabotage, and social anxiety.

3. Secrecy

The final aspect that feeds shame is secrecy. When we experience shame or a deep sense of self-imposed humiliation, the tendency or the inclination is to run away and hide. When I ask my clients what the experience of shame feels like for them, they often say things like, "I want to hide my face behind my hands," or "I want to just disappear." And it's this exact reaction, this intense fear of being exposed, that causes us to keep our shame a secret.

But when we keep something a secret, it perpetuates the idea that it *must be bad*. If it wasn't bad, why would we feel the need to hide it? And that's why secrecy makes shame bigger.

The opposite of secrecy is to normalise something. To allow it to just be as it is. To realise that we all feel shame in some way and therefore it isn't some big secret but rather a very common occurrence of the human experience. Shame is usually a perception formed during youth, from a very natural and normal desire to be loved and accepted. When this desire is threatened or questioned (whether it be due to a caregiver ignoring or abusing you or a group of kids at school bullying you), the meaning we attach to that experience is that *we* are the ones who are flawed. Otherwise, it would not have happened. Remember, when we are young we don't have the ability to understand that we were ignored or bullied for reasons that usually have much more to do with the other person than with who we are.

And so the shame seed is planted, and it starts to grow. It grows because we never talk about it, we rarely seek help to understand it, and we don't ask others if they feel the same way. Our inner critic is freaked out by it, so reminds us every second of the day about it, and our brain's tendency for negative bias seeks out more reasons to prove it to be true. Gosh, it's exhausting just writing that all out! Can you feel just how heavy shame is to carry? And when it's carried in secret, it becomes a huge burden and a darkness that is difficult to escape. It's this very aspect of shame that fuels destructive behaviours such as self-harm, eating disorders, suicidal ideation, and addiction. These are essentially all attempts to temporarily (or permanently) avoid, deny, control, or find relief from the pain that we feel inside.

Thinking back to Step 1 of this book, you might be able to pinpoint where your own shame story was born. If you're thinking, *I don't have any shame*, that would also mean that you don't ever feel not good enough (and probably don't need to be reading this book).

Thinking that you're not enough in any aspect of your life *is* shame. For some people it might just be bigger and more prominent than others.

This is your opportunity to become aware of your shame and to understand its origins. Remember that the more we understand something, the less scary it becomes. When we understand our own shame and become aware that it is not ultimately true, we can start to quieten the critic, speak up about our shame, and look at practices such as cognitive restructuring, meditation, and self-compassion techniques to help us overcome it. And don't worry, these tools and practices will be shared with you in Step 3.

Journal Questions

* Where in my life do I feel not good enough?
* How does this feeling show up in my actions or behaviours (think about how it may limit you, block you, or create situations where your boundaries may be crossed)?
* If I asked somebody close to me if they agreed that I wasn't good enough in these areas, would they agree? What would they say?
* Is my shame story true? Or do I entertain this thought/feeling out of habit?
* If my shame story didn't exist, how would it change my life? What would be different?

Take your time with these questions as they do require adequate self-inquiry and an ability to think more objectively— to be able to broaden your perspective and your imagination so you can feel what your life would be like without some of the limiting stories you tell yourself. When we assume that all our thoughts are true and real—especially the limiting ones—they can really limit the quality of our life. Imagining a life without those thoughts might feel difficult to do at first, but it's possible. Let me share with you Sarah's story. Sarah is a marketing executive who had been struggling with deep-seated feelings of inadequacy for quite some time.

Despite her impressive accomplishments, Sarah carried a pervasive sense of self-doubt and fear of failure, as though she was constantly waiting for validation from others, fearing that she would never measure up. A common case of imposter syndrome.

In her professional life, Sarah's self-doubt manifested as a reluctance to assert herself in meetings and a hesitation to pursue leadership opportunities, even though she was more than capable. Despite external recognition of her capabilities, Sarah struggled to internalise the praise, convinced that she was not deserving of success.

However, those closest to Sarah saw her in a different light. They admired her resilience, creativity, and unwavering dedication to her work. To them, Sarah was a shining example of competence and professionalism. There was so much evidence to prove her shame story to be untrue.

Throughout our therapeutic journey together, Sarah bravely confronted the beliefs that had been holding her back. We delved into the origins of her feelings of inadequacy, exploring how early experiences may have shaped her self-perception. Together, we challenged the validity of her shame story, encouraging her to recognise her inherent worth and potential.

She began to envision a life free from the constraints of her limiting beliefs. With time, she began to lean in to trusting in her abilities, speaking up with newfound confidence, and seizing opportunities for growth (even though they still felt a little scary). Although the journey is never without challenges, Sarah's progress serves as a reminder that it's all possible: Our thoughts aren't always true, and we do have the ability to change them to work in our favour.

STEP 2

Lesson 7

Perfectionism and Its Love Affair with Shame

Hopefully, it has become clear to you that when we feel as though we are inherently flawed, we can become obsessed with doing anything and everything to prevent that "flaw" being exposed to the world. This obsession, driven by fear, is what we call *perfectionism*. Perfectionism and shame are like best friends, and the pursuit of perfectionism is a dangerous road to travel simply because a perfect human does not exist. The attempt to become perfect will always result in disappointment and perpetuate the story that you are flawed. It's a vicious cycle, to say the least.

Perfectionism is an interesting symptom to understand. I call it a symptom because there is, in my opinion, a cause to this behaviour... and if you haven't guessed already, it's shame.

I have worked with hundreds of clients who present with perfectionistic tendencies. Although everybody's shame story will be slightly different, there are some common behaviours that might feel familiar to you. The hiding of the parts of ourselves that we believe to be flawed. The pretending to be fine or have it all together when perhaps we are breaking inside. The fear of getting it wrong. The fear of being a burden. Just fear—so much fear.

My perfectionism was very wrapped up in the fear of being a burden on others. I held the belief for a long time that being emotional is bad and that my emotions are an inconvenience to others. And so, my perfectionistic mask was to always be fine. My coping mechanism was to be hyper-independent. To never have to rely on others. To be capable by myself. To hold it all together. To keep it all inside. And although these coping mechanisms have their perks (I am a fabulous multitasker, I am self-sufficient, and I am highly capable) they also came with the downside that no one really knew about or saw. The constant pressure to do well. The fear of getting something wrong and having no one to turn to. The feelings of loneliness. The overwhelm of having to carry it all by myself.

As I write about my own experiences with perfectionism, I can feel the constriction within my body as it recalls the feelings and beliefs it once had. If you resonate at all, and before we take a closer look at what the research tells us about perfectionist tendencies, let's take a mindful pause to recentre and release.

Mindful Check-In

The following practice is one I have adapted from Peter Levine's "Compassionate Self Holding Exercise". Sometimes when we feel alone, or under pressure, or like we can't ask for help, the body can start to feel tense, tight, and stressed. We long for someone to be there with us, but perhaps there is no one around to lean on or to help us soothe. This beautiful practice reminds us of the nurturing support we can offer ourselves during these moments. By simply placing our hands on our body in different locations, we can embody the sensation of being supported.

* Start in a comfortable seated position and close your eyes if it feels safe to do so. If not, then simply lower your gaze.
* To begin, place both hands on your heart and bring something or someone to mind who makes

you feel loved and supported. This could be a person, a pet, or even a place that makes your body feel safe and your heart feel open.

* Notice how the feeling impacts the heart, and imagine that this feeling glows a warm golden colour radiating from your heart into the palms of your hands, almost as if you are charging your hands with the love from your heart.

* Next, take your hands and place them on either side of your head. Breathe here slowly and mindfully for 5 full breaths.

* Take one hand and place it on your forehead, and place the other at the base of your skull. Breathe here slowly and mindfully for 5 full breaths.

* Keep the one hand on your forehead and move the other onto your heart. Breathe here slowly and mindfully for 5 full breaths.

* Take the hand from your forehead and place it on your belly whilst leaving the other hand on your heart. Breathe here slowly and mindfully for 5 full breaths.

* Take the hand from your heart and place it back on the base of your skull whilst keeping the other hand on your belly. Breathe here slowly and mindfully for 5 full breaths.

* Take both hands out to your sides, and on the exhale wrap them around your body as if giving yourself a big hug. Stay here a moment or sway the body side to side for extra comfort.

✳ When you're ready you can open your eyes and return to the book.

Hopefully after that compassionate check-in you are feeling a little more held and supported as we navigate the next part of what it means to be a perfectionist.

Researchers Paul Hewitt and Gordon Flett were the first to really decipher and understand perfectionistic tendencies back in 1991. What they found was that perfectionism can be broken down into three different types.

1. Self-Orientated Perfectionism

Self-orientated perfectionism is when the expectation to be perfect comes from the self. High expectations of ourselves drive our desire to be flawless. This type of perfectionism isn't necessarily a bad thing in moderate doses. It allows us to achieve goals, hold high performance standards, remain driven during times of adversity, and aim for a productive and successful life or career. It becomes dangerous when the expectations are so high that it impedes happiness.

A self-orientated perfectionist may feel shame when they make an error at work, forget to do something, or fail to achieve a goal or task exactly when and how they expected to. Their inner belief that they must always do everything correctly the first time leaves no room for human error. It doesn't allow space for needed things in life, such as rest, healing after getting the flu, spending quality time with one's spouse or kids, or enjoying a holiday.

Furthermore, there might be a tendency to keep shifting one's goalposts. A self-orientated perfectionist may experience perpetual dissatisfaction once they achieve a goal because it hasn't given them the sense of accomplishment they were seeking (or the sense of accomplishment was only short-lived). And so the wheel keeps turning and they keep running. Hello, burnout and utter exhaustion. I see a lot of myself when I read through this description.

2. Other Orientated Perfectionism

The opposite of self-orientated perfectionism is when we have the same high expectations of flawlessness, but instead of being directed at self, they are directed at everyone else.

The pressure here falls on the other person whilst we are left either feeling as though we can't trust anybody to do things "right" or consistently feeling annoyance and disappointment in humanity.

Adopting this style of behaviour makes it difficult to accept other people's humanness and to allow for the fact that other people think, work, and behave very differently from you. The "my way or the highway" attitude makes it challenging to foster healthy relationships and will often lead to arguments or conflict around topics of control and unmet expectations. It's normal for this person to be left feeling resentful, irritated, and annoyed because of their unmet expectations and rigid approach to life. It's also a sure way to push people away, because they wind up feeling that they can never make you happy, regardless how hard they try.

3. Socially Prescribed Perfectionism

Last, we have socially prescribed perfectionism. This is a style of perfectionism that researchers consider the most dangerous for our mental health and sense of self-worth, as well as being the most interlinked with eating disorders and addiction.

Socially prescribed perfectionism is when a person's worthiness is held up against the *perception* of what other people think of or expect of them. They look at society's expectations of "perfect" and strive to meet that. This could be society's views of the perfect body, the perfect family, the perfect way of parenting, the perfect career, or the perfect amount of money. With the exposure to magazines, billboards, targeted online advertising, social media obsession, and the like, there is no shortage of pressure.

A quick story on socially prescribed perfectionism...

I think back to my teenage years and early twenties living in Australia, in an affluent area known as The Golden Triangle. Although my friends and colleagues were genuinely kind and remarkable individuals, there was an undeniable pressure within the community to conform to a certain lifestyle. This manifested in expectations of being in relationships with partners who shared similar backgrounds, residing in specific suburbs with picturesque homes and luxury vehicles, and indulging in extravagant vacations and possessions such as boats and holiday houses.

Although I cherish many fond memories from that period of my life and harbour no ill will toward those who enjoy privileged lifestyles, it's important to acknowledge the pervasive influence of societal norms. The pressure to uphold a cookie-cutter image of success was palpable, fuelled by gossip and a subtle undercurrent of elitism. While outwardly denying judgement of others, many succumbed to the unspoken expectation of material wealth and social status, me included.

Living within this environment, I witnessed firsthand the impact of socially prescribed perfectionism on individuals' self-esteem and sense of worth. Despite the facade of affluence and contentment, there was an underlying sense of pressure to conform. Looking back, I recognise why I felt a sense of unease a lot of the time: I wasn't being authentic, and many of the values within that community were simply not the values I personally held. It's not that my values are right and theirs are wrong, it's just that I was trying to fit in a space which wasn't really "me". The importance of authenticity and self-acceptance in navigating societal expectations and forging genuine connections beyond materialistic ideals became increasingly important to me the older I got.

It's no surprise that despite being given incredible opportunities, a significant number of people I know experimented with heavy drug abuse, lived in broken families, suffered with anger management issues, and many experienced high levels of anxiety and depression. The bullying and issues experienced within the private schools also bred a lot of shame, specifically among men. Overall, there was a lot of secrecy between friends, a lot of backstabbing and infidelity. There were also more cases of drug overdose and suicide than I'd like to think, starting from as young as 15 years old. From the outside this world looked like a utopia, but once you looked a little deeper, you could see the cracks, which existed because many people struggled to maintain such expectations and ways of living.

I always felt like an outsider despite my many wonderful friends and despite doing well at school. It's like something always felt a little off. I could feel myself succumbing to many of the same beliefs and behaviours, often doing things that did not align with my values because I wanted to fit in, too. It wasn't until my late twenties that I made the radical decision to pack up my life of 15 years and move back home to Indonesia where I grew up.

You may read these three types of perfectionism and think, *Wow, I resonate with all of these...is that even possible?* The answer is yes, it is. Although some of us may have a tendency toward one style only, I have worked with many individuals who demonstrate all three. And what a burden that is to carry! Can you imagine? The weight is incredible.

Unfortunately, we know from recent research conducted by Thomas Curran and Andrew Hill that not only is perfectionism dangerous for one's mental health, but it has actually increased significantly over the past thirty years. More and more people are battling with the innate feeling of never being good enough, resulting in a more anxious, more shameful, and less authentic humanity.

In my opinion, the consequence of perfectionistic thinking can result in three very different ways of being. Sometimes a person will move through all these experiences, whereas others may gravitate toward just one. See which resonates the most for you.

1. We don't stop running

We keep running toward our definition of perfect, like mice on a wheel. We tell ourselves that "as soon as I buy that thing" or "as soon as I get this one lip filler" or "as soon as I start my diet" then we'll be good. Then we get there, and we look around...and we start comparing ourselves to others. What we see is that Jane over there has more lip filler than we have and looks waaaaay better, or how Sarah put up a story on Instagram saying that the diet we are currently on isn't that good and that she prefers something else. "F**K! I've done it wrong... again. I'm such an idiot, everyone's going to think I'm such an idiot." And so we keep running, chasing, showing up as someone who isn't who we are, and doing things we actually don't really want to do just so that we fit in. And you know what we feel? We feel exhausted. But the option of being ourselves just isn't an option because that isn't good enough, remember?

2. We self-sabotage

When we have a lack of self-worth, a relentless inner critic, or a mindset geared toward perfectionistic thinking, we may start to self-sabotage. To self-sabotage means to hinder our chances of success, love, growth, connection, or opportunity. We might reject a romantic partner before they can reject us (even if things are going really well). We might start slacking off at work once we realise a promotion could be on the horizon. This can be done consciously or unconsciously: Some people don't even realise that they are engaging in behaviour preventing them from living a full life. These behaviours are designed to keep us protected from the pain of failure, the pain of rejection, or the pain of being reminded that if something does go wrong, our beliefs of unworthiness are, in fact, true. Self-sabotage is a form of control as it allows a person to some extent predict the future.

> Remember that it's not actually about being "perfect" but rather about the fear beneath the behaviour.

3. We paralyse and self-destruct

This option is triggered by the fear that if it doesn't go perfectly the first time, we are immediately a failure, an outcast, or a laughing-stock. So instead of trying at all, we literally do nothing. We freeze. Procrastination and paralysis are common side effects of perfectionism. This can lead to even more shame, guilt, and resentment than the first option. Sitting and doing nothing, watching your life go by and wishing you had the courage to at least try can make the inner critic *so loud*. This can segue into feelings of deep depression and even addictive tendencies. We might learn that the only way to deal with the voices in our head or the anxiety keeping us up at night is to drink it away, smoke it away, shop it away, or eat it away. Anything that gives us temporary relief is good enough for now, isn't it?

Exploring the fact that we all hold some type of perfectionistic tendency is a fascinating self-inquiry process. Remember that it's not actually about being "perfect" but rather about the fear beneath the behaviour. This is why perfectionism can look different in everyone; it all depends on the story they tell themselves and the fear that drives their choices or lack thereof. On the following page you will find a series of self-reflection questions for you to journal about in relation to this topic. Unless we actively learn to understand ourselves, we can't make the changes necessary to soothe the fear and shift gear toward a lifestyle that feels more aligned and more authentic. And remember that the *how* is coming soon... We are still understanding how it all fits together, but in the chapters to come you'll discover ways to address your perfectionistic tendencies with tenderness and compassion.

Journal Questions

* When I consider my own beliefs and behaviours, which ones are driven by the fear of not fitting in, of being exposed, or come from a place where shame sits in the driver's seat?
* What behaviours do I engage in that don't align with my values or who I want to be?
* If I were to stop acting this way and start acting like the "real" me, what am I afraid might happen?
* Is this fear valid? If the worst happened, do I think that I may be able to navigate through it and be okay five years from now?
* How would my life feel and look different if I were to let go of the pressure and expectations I place on myself and embraced the person I truly want to be?

Lesson 8

How We Use Food (and Other Things) to Self-Soothe

So far, we have explored the beliefs and values that shape us both from childhood and society, understood our traumatic experiences, seen the way in which our need for meaning creates thoughts that perpetuate our shame stories, and looked at what perfectionism truly means.

Now I want to talk to you about how most people don't understand all of this, but how they do *feel* the pain of it all. When we feel pain or discomfort but don't understand its origins, it becomes even more difficult to manage and arguably even more painful. And in our lack of understanding, we naturally want to find a quick fix, right? Some form of relief... anything really.

When I worked as a nutritionist, I predominantly treated women who had severe gut issues and experienced high levels of stress and anxiety. In many instances this stress and anxiety resulted in disordered eating behaviours, and sometimes eating disorders so severe they needed to be hospitalised. Later, as a therapist, I began by working within the field of drug and alcohol addiction. From these experiences, it became evident to me that addiction toward anything (inclusive of food) usually occurs as an unconscious attempt to soothe emotions and sensations that we just don't know how to deal with in a healthy way.

When we don't have the tools to safely and healthily navigate our feelings of stress or shame or not-good-enough, we can get hooked on a cycle of numbing via self-destructive behaviours, even if logically we know it's not good for us. As a nutritionist and as a therapist, I have seen the consequences of self-destruction. It can look like hospitalisation due to anorexia, a destroyed gastrointestinal tract due to excessive vomiting and laxative use, obesity and its associated health issues, cutting oneself or other forms of self-harm, and rehabilitation due to drug and alcohol abuse. Though you might be thinking this is all quite extreme, it's also important to not turn a blind eye to where our shame and lack of self-awareness can take us.

So, if they are so destructive, why do we use these substances or behaviours to regulate our feelings of inadequacy? To understand why a person does anything, we need to understand what their chosen unhealthy habit or addiction gives them, and how it might remedy their emotional pain and suffering even if they know that it's bad for them. Through this understanding, we see what might be lacking or missing in their life. Dr Gabor Maté believes it's important to always ask the question: "not why the addiction, but why the pain?" It's typical that many people only see the symptom or the destructive behaviour and then make assumptions about that person being bad or wrong or somehow an inconvenience to society. It's typical that many people are afraid of what they see when a loved one is engaging in destructive patterns and that they may want them to fix it quickly by means of medication. It's typical that many people feel so uncomfortable when someone they know is suffering that they choose to simply cut them out of their lives because they can't deal with what they see or the repercussions on their relationship. Although all these responses are understandable, none involves someone asking "why are you in pain in the first place?" The behaviour is just the band-aid to a much deeper, personal issue which, if you haven't already guessed, requires awareness, understanding, connection, validation and self-regulation to be healed. Only then will that person no longer need the band-aid.

I'll never forget one young woman who came into the rehab clinic where I was working. All the people I met there have a place in my heart, but she impacted me more emotionally than others. She was young, just 21 at the time. When she came in she could hardly speak... She was still so drugged up and the substances within her system were still wearing off. She had scabs all over her skin from picking and itching (a side effect of using methamphetamines). Her teeth were dark. She was quite literally a shell of a human, and it broke my heart. For a week she moved in and out of this dissociative state, not really wanting to engage with the rest of the group, moving through feelings of anger and defensiveness and often pushing away any attempt at help or connection. She stayed with us longer than others did, nearly three months. Her addiction had taken her to some very dark places and, sadly, she had experienced some very difficult things no young woman should have to experience. But she did the work. She did not turn away from her pain. Slowly but surely, with the support of the incredible team of professionals, she was able to develop the tools, techniques, and knowledge to heal herself. I remember walking into work one morning a few days before she was due to be picked up by her parents, and she was swimming in the pool. She climbed out when I arrived, frangipani in her hair, big smile on her face. And she ran up to me and hugged me good morning. She had a lightness in her step, a playfulness in her voice, and she was happy... genuinely happy. I could see it, feel it, and sense it in her entire being. It brings me to tears when I even write about it because she is one of the reasons why I believe so much in this work. Watching her transformation gave me faith in humanity and truly cemented the belief I hold so dear, which is that all people are inherently good. We are born inherently good and worthy; it's life and our conditioning and lack of proper support that can take us down the wrong paths.

If I feel as though life is depressing or meaningless, I might be drawn to something that gives me a sense of being alive: sugar, cocaine, speed, methamphetamines, or caffeine. If I get stuck in the never-ending loop of my thoughts, I might seek something that gives me a feeling of relief, dissociation, or numbness, such as alcohol, marijuana, sedatives, sleeping tablets. If I feel as though my life is out of control, I would naturally gravitate toward something that gives me a heightened sense of control, such as restrictive eating, dieting, fasting, dexamphetamines. It makes sense, right? If I don't have the tools internally to navigate these feelings, but I find something else that does it for me, it's easy to see how quickly that thing will become a habit or possibly even turn into an addiction.

Before we delve any deeper, it's important here to clarify what addiction is and how it may be different from just an unhealthy habit. Regardless of which definition you look at, the common indicator of an addict is that they *know* what they are doing is destructive and harmful to themselves or others, and yet they *still* engage in the activity. An unhealthy habit, on the other hand, is something we can actively stop doing on our own once we realise that it's becoming unhealthy or dangerous in some way.

So, what about food? I get asked this question a lot and I work with many, many clients who turn to food as a means for regulation. Emotional eating, binge-eating, purging, restriction, yo-yo dieting? Each of these issues is multilayered, and as you know by now, the environment, values, ideals, and behaviours imposed upon us or

> To understand why a person does anything, we need to understand what their chosen unhealthy habit or addiction gives them, and how it might remedy their emotional pain and suffering even if they know that it's bad for them.

acted out around us will form much of the way we use and see food (as well as our bodies). Couple that with any other feelings of disconnection or inadequacy, and food can quickly become a substance we learn to manipulate to consciously or unconsciously make us feel better temporarily.

Something becomes habitual or even addictive because certain foods and behaviours affect the chemical processes in the body that send signals to the brain. The neurotransmitter dopamine, in particular, is a chemical associated with pleasure and reward, and results in us experiencing a rush of feel-good emotions, a sense of relief, and temporary euphoria. Dopamine is intertwined with our relationship to food as it is also responsible for our hunger and satiety cues. Interestingly, much like certain recreational drugs, salt, fat, and sugar can also boost our dopamine receptors. This means eating these things makes us feel good, which is why we gravitate to eating more junk food than salads when we're feeling down or stressed. Makes sense, right? Who wants a salad when they feel sad? We usually want pasta or fries or a tub of ice cream. Don't get me wrong, I don't think there is anything wrong with comfort eating every now and then... I do it, too, when I feel down or stressed. Where it becomes a problem is when we aren't actively doing anything about the way that we feel and we *solely* rely on the food to "fix" our situation.

If we don't do anything about the way we feel, the brain will want to seek out *more* comfort by eating *more* of those same things. The food becomes a readily available quick fix, much more appealing than the in-depth journey it might take a person to properly understand and regulate their emotional landscape. This pattern is what many call comfort eating, emotional eating, or stress eating. It doesn't have to be an issue unless it becomes the *only way* someone regulates their emotions. If this happens, the behaviour can quickly become a segue for intense binge-eating cycles, heightened levels of shame, and possibly bulimia. What makes bulimia different from binge-eating is that there is a purge involved. Usually, in the case of bulimia, someone will initially binge to deal with their difficult emotions, but by doing so they quickly feel intense guilt and even more shame, which then results in wanting to throw up. The action of throwing up subsequently provides another feeling of temporary relief and another dopamine hit.

Interestingly, restriction of food can *also* cause a rush of reward and flood us with temporary positive emotions because a person may associate the *act* of eating with being bad, wrong, or shameful. Therefore, the withholding of food ignites the same reward response. How many of you have felt incredible amounts of satisfaction when you've embarked on a calorie-counting diet? Or become obsessive about a number on the scales? Or with dissecting the menu of any restaurant you go to? Food restriction is, in most cases I have worked with, interlinked with a person's desire to feel in control. Perhaps when they were younger they lived in a chaotic environment, or perhaps something happened to them which they had no control over. This can feel incredibly scary to a person's nervous system and so anything that brings that sense of control back will feel soothing. As you can see, how someone uses food as a tool for relief will depend on the person's perspective of food, their relationship with their body, their ability to regulate difficult emotions, and their unique shame story.

One person's unhelpful habit can be another person's kryptonite, which is why we will all have different go-to habits regarding what we might do or how we might act. The substance or behaviour will usually be something that provides us with the exact feeling we are needing. This is why some people will turn to alcohol whereas others will turn to speed. Why one person might become obsessive about exercise and another person addicted to gambling. It's unique because we are unique. Once the connection has been made and a habit is formed, the risk of addiction becomes more prevalent as it is coupled with our increase in tolerance for the behaviour or substance.

One of the other issues with this fixation on seeking temporary pleasure is that we aren't seeking reward or happiness from within ourselves or from any other area of our lives, which also stimulate hormones and neurotransmitters capable of making us feel things like joy, trust, bonding, and relief. Yes, you read correctly. It isn't *just* dopamine that makes us feel good! In fact, relying on dopamine alone to fuel your happiness just won't cut it as it only has a short-term effect on the brain, hence its addictive nature.

Here are a few of the other hormones and neurotransmitters responsible for making us feel good:

Serotonin is known as the *true* happiness hormone due to its long-term effects on the brain and its ability to stabilise your moods and enhance feelings of contentment. It also plays a crucial role in regulating your sleep pattern and digestive system functioning. In fact, a huge proportion of serotonin (over 90 percent!) is actually made by the bacteria found within your gastrointestinal tract, hence the reason why poor diet and issues such as Irritable

Bowel Syndrome (IBS) can have such a significant effect on your mood and increase the likelihood of depression and anxiety. The solution? First, by looking after your digestive health and eating a wholefoods diet rich in starches, fibres, and plants, you will be supporting the ecosystem of the bacteria within your gut responsible for the production of these happy hormones. Second, engaging in activities such as spending time in the sunshine, meditation, yoga, and connecting with nature can all have a positive influence on your production and release of serotonin.

Oxytocin, also known as the love or cuddle hormone. Oxytocin enhances feelings of bonding, trust, love, and connection. It also reduces stress. It's closely associated with your senses and can be enhanced through cuddling, sexual intimacy, holding hands, laughing, patting an animal, expressing gratitude, cooking, enjoying a meal with friends or a loved one, and getting (or giving) a massage.

Endorphins You'd probably be familiar with the effects of endorphins every time you finish a workout or a long run. It's also known as the hormone that gives you the "runner's high" and cleverly helps your body relax and relieve pain, which is why it is released during or after times of strenuous exercise or physical activity. Encourage your body to release more endorphins through daily exercise, dancing, joining a spin class, or simply getting outside and moving your body more!

If we can focus on hacking all these hormones (especially serotonin), we reduce the yo-yo effect of the intense highs and lows, which might be prevalent if we were to purely engage in things that cause temporary pleasure and reward.

As usual, here are a few questions for you to start your own self-inquiry process around this topic. Although you may not be in the depths of an addiction, you may notice how you habitually turn to certain behaviours to avoid, deny, or suppress certain discomforts that lie within you.

Journal Questions

* What's my go-to unhelpful habit when I feel overwhelmed with emotion?
* What does this person/substance/food give me, or how does it make me feel when I use it/do it?
* If I didn't have this thing to help me navigate my emotions, what do I think would happen to me?
* Knowing that I wasn't given all the tools of self-regulation as a child, what words of compassion could I offer myself right now to help me not hold guilt or remorse toward myself and instead encourage me to seek development in this area?

Step 3

Reconnection

You might be thinking, *Okay, all this information is getting a bit overwhelming. I understand it now, but what do I do about it?* Welcome to Step 3! Throughout the rest of this book, you will learn some of my favourite tools for reconnection and healing to help you find a deeper sense of self-acceptance and, eventually, a feeling of inner peace.

This step is called Reconnection because ultimately that's what the wounded parts of us need more than anything. Trauma and toxic stress create disconnection, from ourselves as well as from others. It also creates a sense of disempowerment and a lack of internal safety. So, healing is about re-establishing connection, empowerment, and safety.

The theories, lessons, and tools found in this step are the same ones I would invite you to do and practice if you were a client of mine. They have been fine-tuned over years and years of working with hundreds of clients, and I hope that you, too, will find them useful and transformative. I feel immensely grateful that I have worked with the physiology of the body as a nutritionist, with the complexity of the mind as a therapist, and with the energetics of the subtle body as a yoga teacher. It's proved a very useful trifecta for helping my clients address all aspects of mind, body, and spirit. When it comes to self-development, I really don't believe that we can address just one part of who we are. Each part is connected to another, and focusing on one means neglecting the other and possibly just transferring the pain or confusion to a different location.

So, let's dive in, shall we? Remember, these tools are designed to be contemplated and practiced over time, consistently and persistently. This means we require patience with ourselves... True healing is not achieved via quick-fix solutions, and the journey back to self is usually a long, winding road often filled with little roadblocks and U-turns. It takes time because the brain and body require time and repetition to become familiar with a new normal.

> Healing is about re-establishing connection, empowerment, and safety.

New beliefs, new behaviours, new sensations in the body. It takes time to trust that fears or limiting beliefs are no longer true. It takes time to get unstuck from a nervous system that is used to bracing for the worst.

It's normal to take two steps forward and one step back. It's normal to feel fed up from time to time. It's normal to still get triggered. It's normal to have days where you just can't be bothered. Keep going and keep applying the techniques you read here. Trust me when I say that they will help, as I have seen them help so many before you.

Lesson 9

Nurturing and Validating Ourselves

One of the ways in which we can feel more connected with ourselves is to learn how to better accept ourselves, as we are. Eek! That might feel daunting. How can we accept something that we believe is bad or flawed or wrong? I hope that by now, you know you are not inherently flawed and you realise that you are a human being acting and living and behaving in a way that is a result of your lived experiences and conditioning. That's all it is. You're not bad or wrong. You're human.

Cultivating more self-acceptance means learning to be okay with the parts of yourself you criticise, hide, or feel ashamed of. It's the opposite of self-criticism. The simplest path to self-acceptance involves understanding the origins of the traits you may dislike about yourself. And remembering that many of these aspects develop as learned behaviours, coping mechanisms, and adaptations to your upbringing and the beliefs you've formed over time.

Once again, you aren't wrong or bad for being a reactive person, or for having perfectionist tendencies, or for being terrified of your own feelings. You aren't bad or wrong for binge drinking or binge eating if you don't know any other way to cope. These are just *symptoms* of your lived experiences. They make sense. You learned how to be this way because it's what kept you safe and attached once upon a time.

I'm going to say that again so that it really sinks in:

> You learned how to be this way because it kept you safe and attached once upon a time.

So, instead of hating on yourself, can you learn to make space to foster deeper self-understanding? Can you learn to possibly even embrace these parts of you and be in awe of yourself because of how you have managed to cope until now? When we can learn to understand, accept, and validate ourselves we become more integrated as a human—more connected.

It's a different way of looking at things, I know, but it's a practice that really calms those wounded parts within us. We all have sub-personalities that dictate much of the way we operate. In therapy, the exploration of these sub-personalities is what we would refer to as "parts work." This is an approach that involves working with different parts of a person's psyche or personality to understand and resolve inner conflicts, trauma, and emotional distress. It's based on the idea that we all have different aspects of ourselves that may have competing desires, beliefs, and emotions.

Some of the common "parts" or sub-personalities you may be familiar with already are the inner critic, the inner child, and the higher self. We've visited the inner critic in Step 2. It's the part that critiques our every move due to fear of being exposed, shamed, or hurt. It's the voice that drives the perfectionistic tendencies, the one that tells you that you're not good enough, and ultimately the one that governs a huge part of how you portray yourself publicly. You might remember that the inner critic's sole purpose is protection. She is like a micromanager dissecting your every move so you don't embarrass yourself or do something that may threaten your sense of belonging. Although the inner critic may be harsh in the way she communicates, ultimately what she feels is fear. She is just super scared. Does that make sense? And usually, if you can see her in this light and understand her core emotion of fear, you can also come to the realisation that she is utterly exhausted. She doesn't want to be micromanaging constantly. She wants to feel safe, at ease, at peace... but she can't. She has no one telling her that it's all going to be OK. Every single client I have worked with, when they develop the ability to see the different parts of themselves as separate characters, has come to understand so much more about them and learn how to respond to them so differently.

Exercise

BEFRIENDING YOUR INNER CRITIC

Let's get to know your inner critic as if she (or he) were a completely separate person. Grab your journal and explore with me.

1. Close your eyes and connect to the part of you that is self-critical. This shouldn't be hard to do. Just think of the last time you said something negative about yourself or belittled yourself. Find that voice and stay with it.

2. Now get curious. Imagine you are meeting this person for the very first time and you want to know all about them. Get as creative as you need to when you answer the following questions.
   - Where in your body does the inner critic reside?
   - How do you know when it is present? What sensations do you feel in your body?
   - What does it look like? Can you identify its gender, age, colours, clothing, facial expressions?
   - What does it sound like? Connect with its tone, pitch, frequency of the way it sounds when it speaks.

3. Once you have developed a clear image of your inner critic it will be much easier to communicate with it because you see it as something separate from yourself.
4. As strange as this may sound, try to communicate with it, asking the following questions and just seeing what answers arise. Go with it, follow your intuition, and write down anything that comes up. There is no right or wrong with this exercise.
   - Why do you criticise and belittle me?
   - What are you afraid of?
   - How are you trying to protect me?
   - What else do you want me to know?
5. The final piece of this self-inquiry is to discover the needs of your inner critic. What is going to help it feel at ease? Safe? Secure? At peace? Ask it what it needs from you to feel relief, and see what it says.

In my experience of working with many people's inner critics, the most common needs that arise are the need for trust, the need for understanding, and the sensation within the body of safety, a knowing that regardless of what happens, you will be OK. Is this what came up for you, too? Usually what the critic really wants is for someone else to take over. Someone who it can rely on. If you haven't already guessed, this person is *you*. The adult you. The higher self you. The wiser, more compassionate you. The one who logically knows that so many of the fears and worries of the critic are simply not true. Your inner critic needs you to take over. To step up and lead the way.

And what of the inner child? If you're wondering who the inner child is, it's the version of you who quite literally is still showing up as if your childhood experiences are still happening for you now, in real time. The version of you who holds all the shame from your childhood and who often still acts out in childish ways. It's the part of you who the inner critic is trying so hard to protect.

For example, you may notice that when you have an argument with your partner, you storm off and slam doors, or when you don't get your way you quite literally throw a tantrum. Perhaps in social situations you become incredibly shy and afraid, or find yourself harbouring intense feelings of being unprotected, unloved, unseen, or unsafe. Maybe you spend your life always trying to make other people happy because you feel like everything is always your fault.

We all have an inner child. In fact, getting to know and understand my own inner child was probably the most effective part of my entire self-development journey. It's likely that your inner child longs to be properly validated, soothed, loved, and nurtured in all the ways she did not receive when she was younger. Just like with our inner critic, healing the inner child requires meeting its unmet needs. Not through aggression or ignorance or belittlement, as the inner critic attempts to do, but in a way that is more tender and more from the energy of a caring parent.

It's about offering her patience, compassion, acknowledgement, space to be heard, and unconditional love for who she is, as she is. It's also about being proud of her for the way she navigated some of those confusing, chaotic, difficult, or perhaps traumatic events of her life. It requires you remembering her inherent worth and reminding her of that as often as possible.

I invite you to go back and reflect on all the answers you have written for the journal questions so far. Really take it in, as if you are observing someone else's life or story. When reflecting on your own childhood experiences, the invitation is to try to see and understand them from the eyes and mind of a *child*, and not as the adult you are now. We do this to accurately understand how hard some of that stuff would have been to navigate for a person who has only been on this earth a few years. It's quite incredible that she was clever enough to adapt the way she did.

Sometimes it can be hard to imagine our inner child, especially if our memories of childhood are faded. If this is you, try to imagine *any* child you know—perhaps your own child, your niece/nephew, or a child of a friend—and spend a moment reflecting on their innocence and how young they truly are. If you do have clear memories of yourself as a child, I invite you to close your eyes and picture her and her innocence in the same way, or draw upon a photo of your younger self and become reacquainted with her. Another way to reconnect to your inner child can be through a guided meditation that focuses on this subject. You'll need to discover the most effective method of connection for you. And once you meet her and realise that she has a home within you, you can become more curious about when and how she shows up.

Self-Reflection

* What needs did I have as a child that weren't met and how did this make me feel?
* What were the resulting adaptive behaviours that arose because of these unmet needs? Did I become avoidant, defensive, scared, anxious?
* Where do I witness my own childlike behaviours arise in day-to-day situations? Give examples.
* How do I know when my inner child is active? What sensations do I feel in my body?
* How do I currently respond to my inner child? Is it helpful or unhelpful in making her feel seen, heard, loved, safe, and validated?
* What could be a different way of responding to this part of me now that I understand her better?
* When she reacts within me in future, what words/affirmations or actions does she need to hear/do to realise she isn't still stuck in her childhood environment?
* How can I provide her with her unmet needs now as an adult? What would this look like in action?

So, for example, perhaps you grew up in a family where children were to be seen and not heard. Therefore, one of your unmet needs as a child may have been to have your opinion or feelings validated and acknowledged, to have someone give you the time of day to *be* heard and acknowledged. Naturally, it may have made you feel invisible, unimportant, and that what you have to say isn't worthy or interesting. The adaptive behaviours may have looked like becoming very introverted, feeling fearful of speaking up, overthinking everything you say, developing social anxiety, and failing to express or set boundaries with others. All things considered, and in my opinion, it's completely understandable that a person would have adapted her personality like this. Would you agree? You might find that you wish to offer compassion to this newfound understanding in the form of validation, speaking to your inner child and saying something like:

"I know you felt as though you weren't seen or understood. I understand that it has resulted in your introversion, and I am here to ensure you always feel worthy. I am listening and value what you have to say."

In the future, when you feel triggered or react in a way that brings up those familiar feelings of shame, perhaps you could come up with a few simple affirmations to help you get through the moment, such as

"You are safe here."
"Your voice matters."

> "I am here to help you through this."
> "If we don't try, we won't know."
> "I value you."
> "You've got this, I'm right here."

When it comes to meeting her unmet needs now as an adult, some simple tools you might include in your day-to-day life could be

- journaling at the end of each day to reflect on moments when you felt unseen or unheard to increase your self-awareness.
- practicing writing down things you'd like to say or express to others and addressing the fears that arise with compassion from your adult self.
- working with a therapist or coach on using your voice and feeling understood, gaining clarification on self-expression, healthy communication, and improving self-worth.
- cognitive restructuring techniques for overthinking. We explore this a little more in Lesson 11, but basically the term *cognitive restructuring* just refers to the restructuring of our thoughts, replacing the negative or limiting ones with more helpful thoughts that align with the adult we wish to be.
- practicing mirror work: standing or sitting in front of a mirror and practicing saying the things you wish to express to others.

- experimenting with sharing more often with people close to you to boost your sense of safety within a relationship and to disprove your limiting beliefs.

And that's just *one* example of one possible unmet need. It might feel weird at first, the concept of speaking to your inner child in that way or even acknowledging that she exists. But over time and with consistency, this practice not only becomes second nature but also helps you heal wounds that still linger and arise, impacting your day-to-day life. A lot of people don't like the idea of doing inner child work because they have a misconception that it means reliving their childhood trauma and becoming a "victim" to their experiences. There are critics who say that doing inner child work leaves a person riddled with self-pity and the expectation that the world owes them constant coddling and validation. But this is not the purpose of doing inner child work. In fact, thinking that the world owes you pity and validation means that you are *still* stuck in your childlike persona. The purpose of inner child work is simply to recognise that a huge part of you carries the shame, beliefs, and behaviours from your childhood and that it affects who you are and how you operate now, as an adult. It's about developing the awareness of when your inner child is active versus when she's not, so you can differentiate between the two and tend to the wounded parts of yourself as they arise, ensuring that they no longer dictate your life. Inner child work frees you to go about your life as the adult you are *now*, living your life through the lens of your current day values, morals, and beliefs and not through the lens of a dependent infant.

I know that this might seem like a lot of hard work, and to be frank with you, initially it *is*. It takes time to familiarise ourselves with the concept and even more time for our brains to rewire themselves into a new way of thinking and feeling and responding, which is essentially what this theory is all about. By learning to engage more and more from your adult self, you are creating new and more helpful neural pathways in your brain, which changes the way you go about your life.

The term *neuroplasticity* refers to the incredible ability of the brain to form new neural connections across the span of your life and reorganise itself multiple times over depending on what's happening to it. As we learn new things, the brain forms new neural connections to remember and be able to do those things. The common phrase used by many neuroscientists is "what fires together, wires together". Take learning a language or playing an instrument as a basic example. The more you repeat, the better you get because the connection becomes stronger.

When a brain encounters damage or disruption it will naturally become wired for safety or survival, but it can, over time, rewire itself back to functioning from a place of safety and regulation. When we consistently and persistently think and experiment with taking action toward a *new* belief or *new* way of seeing things, we can slowly but surely rewire our brains to disregard the old belief pattern and favour the new one. It is a truly incredible feature of the brain, and we can encourage this process through the incorporation of other techniques such as breathwork, yoga, meditation practices, memory recall, and eye movement desensitisation and reprocessing techniques.

If you have found yourself curious about your own inner child and know for sure that you have childlike parts that may hinder your choices, limit your beliefs, or disrupt your relationships, I would invite you to work with your therapist or a specialist in parts work to explore this topic on a deeper level. Remember that the reason we do the healing work around these sub-personalities is to allow our authentic selves to shine through with confidence, ease, and safety.

Lesson 10

Cultivating Self-Compassion

The second part of reconnection is cultivating self-compassion. Deriving from the Latin word *compati*, compassion literally means "to suffer with." Compassion Focused Therapy (CFT) forms a huge part of my approach to therapy, as does Buddhist psychology, both of which focus deeply on the embodiment of compassion as the gateway to healing. I have spent many years delving into reading, researching, doing courses on, and practicing compassion both toward myself and toward others. I now even teach and run a certification program for practitioners who wish to become Compassion Focused Coaches so they, too, can guide others toward the cultivation of this remarkable quality of self.

Self-compassion has been one of the greatest tools in my own path of healing and self-acceptance, and I hope that it can be yours, too.

I struggled for a long time to truly understand what compassion was, often getting it muddled up with either being overly positive or overly self-pitiful. But compassion isn't about either of those things. It's more about the embodiment of empathy and of being able to meet ourselves or another person where they are at with validation and acceptance. I like to explain self-compassion to my clients as the ability to simply honour our humanness.

One of my favourite books on the topic is *The Places That Scare You*, written by American Tibetan Buddhist Pema Chödrön.

In it she writes: "Compassion is more emotionally challenging than loving-kindness, because it involves the willingness to feel pain. It definitely requires the training of a warrior."

The *willingness* to feel pain. The normalisation of pain and suffering. The acceptance that pain and suffering will be and has always been a huge part of the lived experience. There is relief in that. It means that my pain, my suffering, my experiences, and my past are not to be ashamed of or embarrassed by, but rather to be felt and understood as a normal part of what it means to be human.

As quoted above, to become more compassionate requires the *willingness* to feel pain. Understandably, many people don't want to go there. We are taught to avoid pain, to run away from it, to fear it. And rightly so. Pain is painful. It hurts. It's hard to face. But how are we supposed to empathise with ourselves or others if we don't first see that they are suffering? It's through the suffering that our hearts open up and compassion flows through.

So, what if we learned to view pain differently? To see it as an opportunity for self-inquiry rather than self-destruction? To use it as information that helps us heal? To not move away from it, but toward it? If we could change our perception of pain by normalising the experience of it, it becomes less scary and therefore easier to work with. This can drastically shift our willingness to do the work of healing and self-acceptance.

Indian yoga guru Sadhguru shares that "You can use everything that happens in your life as a process of empowerment, or to entangle yourself." I agree that our pain and suffering can either be a cause for more pain and suffering, or it can be an opportunity for expansion and empowerment. Ultimately, it comes down to perspective.

The truth of the matter is that it's primarily through our pain that we find ourselves. It's through the challenges and difficulties of life that we realise even more who we are, what we value, and how we may need to change. We cannot fully understand ourselves if we don't visit the places that scare us, as it is those places and experiences that also form a huge part of who we are. If we resist acknowledging our own pain, then we resist ourselves and our pain cycle continues. We remain disconnected from ourselves and detached from our path of recovery.

I remember when I first read about the Japanese art of kintsugi, likening it to what self-compassion does for our own suffering and wounding. Kintsugi is when broken pieces of pottery are melded back together with gold, which ultimately creates an even more beautiful piece of art than how it looked before it broke. This repairing process is what happens when we learn how to reconnect to ourselves through self-compassion. It's the honouring of our suffering, our pain, and humanness, tending to those parts of ourselves with tenderness that inevitably helps us grow, learn, and evolve.

The practice of self-compassion looks like treating yourself how you would treat the person you love the most in your life. It's an unconditional acceptance of that person—flaws, mistakes, annoying habits, past experiences, and all. It's about knowing in your heart that they are a worthy being. Worthy of love, worthy of kindness, worthy of your time, worthy of a second chance. If this person

> What if we learned to view pain differently? To see it as an opportunity for self-inquiry rather than self-destruction?

came to you with a problem or a feeling of immense shame around something they had done, I highly doubt that you would perpetuate their shame by telling them what a failure they are or how they should punish themselves for what they have done.

If they told you they hated their body, would you sit with them and spend the next hour nit-picking at their body or calling it disgusting? Or would you empathise with their emotion and perhaps try to help them through what they are experiencing?

I have compiled what I believe are four essential qualities or traits required for a person to become more compassionate toward themselves. These four qualities have come about after having worked with hundreds of clients, helping guide them toward a more self-compassionate state of being. These four qualities are the willingness to be open, the curiosity to explore, the capability for self-validation, and the embodiment of safety.

1. Willingness to see things differently

Starting the journey of self-compassion can feel scary and difficult because, obviously, it requires facing up to and honouring our pain. It also requires us being a heck of a lot kinder to ourselves than we might be used to. Many people who first start this practice feel sceptical about it and naturally want to resist it. So, first, there is the requirement of a willingness to be open. If we approach the work of compassion with a rigid mind or a closed heart, it makes it very difficult to allow ourselves to invite change. If you find yourself in resistance to trying new things, or to understanding yourself in a new way, I'd invite you to explore that resistance. Ask,

- what biases do you have around exploring alternative methods to healing?
- when you think about the prospect of being kinder and more accepting of yourself, what happens?
- what else might get in your way of being open?
- if you aren't willing to change, what's the cost of staying where you are?
- does the cost outweigh the benefit, and, if not, what are you scared of?

2. Curiosity to explore

If we can replace fear, resistance, and judgement with curiosity, we broaden our minds. Instead of saying "This is bad" or "That is wrong", we can say, "Wow, that's interesting... I wonder why it is the way it is?" By asking "why" more often, we find the essential piece of understanding that is required to overcome shame. We realise that we did certain things or have developed certain behaviours not because we are flawed but because of a sequence of experiences that shaped us. Alternatively, we realise that what we are thinking is not even true. It's just a trigger or a memory from the past. And once again, within that comes relief.

Curiosity is also required to do things and try things differently. The things we intuitively *know* our body or mind longs for but which we might have avoided due to fear of judgement or change. The curiosity to explore different ways to heal becomes a gesture of self-respect. It's telling yourself that you are *worthy of healing* regardless of what it takes.

I was recently speaking to a client of mine who has a long history of developmental trauma in relation to her caregivers. She was the victim of both physical and emotional abuse from her father. As a result, her teenage years were very, very difficult as she tried to cope with the shame she felt. She soothed her pain through bingeing and purging, ongoing self-harm, and relying on Xanax to numb her pain. Extreme panic attacks were a regular occurrence. She had been hospitalised more than ten times for various reasons by the time she came to me and understandably felt completely helpless and hopeless about her journey of recovery. She wanted to understand how she could be kinder to herself, and she was willing and ready to try a holistic approach to therapy. She had never explored anything apart from very clinical approaches to her mental health: medication, psychiatric help, hospitalisation, and government rehabilitation. Some of these were helpful, others provided more of a band-aid, not truly addressing the root of her issues.

Over the many months that we worked together, our sessions comprised traditional cognitive behavioural therapy techniques, guided meditation practices, physical yoga practices and somatic coaching, breathwork techniques, and conversation around spirituality and philosophy. We looked at ways to change her lifestyle through her diet and exercise routine and enhanced the quality of her relationships through bettering her communication skills and ability to set boundaries. We worked together for nearly a year, and the woman she was at the end was vastly different to the woman I met when she first contacted me. Confident, content, compassionate, and grounded, she no longer self-harmed; she found a new job she loved; she fell in love with a supportive, kind man who truly values her; and she even embarked on her own yoga teacher training to further her knowledge of the practice.

If she didn't have the willingness to be open and the curiosity to explore, she would not have had the results she did. Even when we feel at our darkest, there is always a tiny glimmer of hope and compassion within our hearts. And that's where we need to focus. It's through this tiny portal that we can find the energy to dedicate ourselves to the inner work of healing and to support ourselves during our setbacks. The more we do it, the more the compassion expands.

3. Embodiment of Self-Validation

The consequence of shame and perfectionism is that we feel as though we are faulty. And if we are faulty, we may become fixated with needing and seeking validation from others. When someone validates us, we feel seen, heard, and understood—three things many humans long for. But placing all our worth in the hands of someone else leaves us in a state of anxiousness. When will I be validated again? What should I do to get their attention? Why haven't I received it yet? To combat this, we need to learn how to validate *ourselves*. This means that when you feel anxious or think a judgemental thought, you normalise it and give it airtime rather than belittling it or criticising it. Once you can normalise the experience you are having, you can access the self-compassionate, wise, and reasonable voice within you to offer guidance. And if you've never come into contact with that voice within you, don't worry, I will provide you with a journaling practice to get you well acquainted.

Engaging with your inner compassionate self is a similar process to speaking to your best friend or loved one if they were to come to you with feelings of inadequacy or shame. I imagine that you wouldn't get angry at them for feeling the way they did, nor would you say things that may make their shame worse. Instead, I assume you'd help them normalise and validate their experience and then offer some sort of guidance or questioning around what they need in order to feel more comfortable with the situation.

Validating inner dialogue sounds like using phrases such as *I understand* and *I can see that you are feeling sad.* It's literally just learning how to speak to yourself in a kinder way. If you're thinking it's weird to speak to yourself, just remember that you do it every day. It's just that you're probably more used to hearing a negative voice rather than a compassionate one, so obviously it will feel unfamiliar at first.

Validation makes it okay to be emotional. Validation makes it okay to be triggered by things: *It's okay to feel scared, I can see how this situation is reminding you of xyz*, or *It's natural that this is causing you to feel avoidant. After all, it's been your protective mechanism for so long.*

Validation allows you to be a *human* when you make mistakes: *I know this feels shit, but we all make mistakes sometimes*, or *It's hard for sure, but we will learn from this, and we can get through it.* Validation helps us navigate things like body shame: *It's okay that you feel a bit uncomfortable in this top; you haven't worn a top like this for a while. What do you need to feel more okay about it?* or *I understand that going to the beach today makes you anxious; we are learning to feel more confident in our body. Perhaps we should bring a sarong as a safety measure to help us navigate this.* Self-validation helps us find the comfort we are seeking and the inner acceptance we always longed for. The quicker we can validate, the quicker our thoughts shift away from over-thinking and move into compassion.

Validating ourselves during times of joy and success is as important as it is during times of struggle or discomfort. To recognise our efforts removes the pressure or expectation that we should be doing *more* or should be doing *better*. If we don't validate ourselves during our triumphs, we risk reinforcing the belief that what we are doing or how we are trying still isn't good enough, when really it is. This is why, during your self-development journey, it's crucial to notice and validate both your wins and your setbacks. The path of knowing and understanding yourself is filled with many twists and turns, setbacks, moments of frustration, and moments of relief, joy, and contentment. Validate it all.

Exercise
STRENGTHENING YOUR COMPASSIONATE VOICE

This exercise usually works well initially as a reflection exercise, so is perhaps ideal to do at the end of the day (until you get used to the flow of it).

Close your eyes and take a few deep breaths to centre the mind. Spend five to ten minutes working backwards, reviewing your day and identifying any times you heard your inner critic. Take a mental note and continue reviewing the day's activities until you reach the morning, when you woke up.

Open your eyes and create two columns on your piece of paper.

MY INNER CRITIC (you could also call it MY HEAD or MY FEARS	MY COMPASSIONATE SELF (you could also call it MY HEART or MY LOVING SELF)

1. First, list everything your inner critic said to you in the left-hand column. This could look like:
   I look shit. Nothing in my wardrobe fits me anymore. He definitely doesn't love me anymore. That's why he was abrupt when I got home.
2. After you have written your list, close your eyes once more and take a few moments to recentre, then focus on a feeling of compassion and kindness, as if you were talking to a best friend, a child, or a loved one.
3. Review each critical statement and reply to yourself with kindness and compassion. Offer your critic understanding, safety, and context. If you get stuck, simply ask yourself, *What advice would I offer my best friend if she said this about herself?*
   For example, if I were to respond to the two critical statements above, I might say:
   It's normal that our bodies change over time. If you don't feel comfortable it doesn't mean you look like shit. Why don't we try something else on which makes us feel more at ease? Could there be another reason why he was abrupt? I know you immediately think it's because he doesn't love you, but your relationship is so loving. We all have bad days and perhaps he's just having a bad day.
4. After the exercise, and if you feel up to it, read out loud the responses you wrote down. The body and mind respond in a very different and positive way when we verbalise these things out loud.

Notice what it feels like to receive these words from yourself to yourself.

5. Keep practicing this exercise every time you feel your inner critic rising strong. Soon enough, you will get into a habit where you start doing it automatically in your own mind.

4. Embodiment of Safety

When we feel truly accepted, understood, and loved, we feel safe. It feels like we can finally breathe a sigh of relief. There's no one we need to try to impress, no second guessing, no reason to be fearful. As you know, shame and perfectionism keep our nervous system in a heightened state of stress, which stimulates either a hyper-aroused or hypo-aroused mind. Our body gets stuck responding to a perceived threat or memory that no longer exists. And because we are stuck in this state, we become over-reactive and easily triggered. We think everyone is out to get us, or everyone is judging us, or a simple conversation is an attack on our character. We are essentially operating from the past in the present moment. And when we find ourselves in these heightened states of reactivity, it can be really hard to think our way out of it.

One of the things we know now, thanks to the research on somatic therapy, is that you can't successfully *think* your way out of stress or anxiety. This is because safety is a sensation that needs to be *felt* in the body and nervous system first before being able to perceive it in the mind. I can *tell* myself that I am safe, but if my heart is still pounding out of my chest, or my breathing is still rapid, my body is going to be sending signals to my brain that it is still under threat. Regardless of what I tell myself, my body needs to feel it, too, on a visceral level.

When we are stressed, our ability for impulse control, to logically process things, to engage in complex decision-making, or to have rational cognitive reasoning is limited. This is because when we are stressed, the amygdala (a part of the brain responsible for activation of the fight-or-flight response) literally hijacks the prefrontal cortex (the part of the brain responsible for rational thought and decision making). It does this to engage our more primal instincts to get away from or be able to fend off the threat. If you think about it, it makes sense and would have been very useful back in the day. Who has time to think when a sabre tooth tiger is about to attack them, right? We don't want to be sitting there weighing the pros and cons of the attack when our life is on the line. The obvious issue nowadays, however, is the fact that in most instances, our life *isn't* on the line.

You may have experienced this hijacking effect of your brain when you're about to engage in a confrontational conversation and you suddenly lose all your words or train of thought. All you want to do is run. Or perhaps you get into an argument with your loved one and say horrible things to them and start slamming doors or punching a wall. You don't mean to do this, but it's as if something has taken over, causing you to act without control. This is all because your prefrontal cortex is not leading the way. Your emotional and survival brain regions are. It's not until you have calmed down that you would be able to reflect on your actions (and probably feel incredibly guilty and confused).

If the prefrontal cortex is not functioning properly in the heat of the moment, then we obviously cannot rely on it to help us effectively. No matter what we say to ourselves, it just won't completely regulate our nervous system because we are speaking to the wrong part of the brain. To self-soothe, we need to rely on doing so through the body. This means focusing on what we call a "bottom-up approach" to feeling safe. Body first, mind second. The way we do this is through sensory awareness and stimulation.

Finding safety within the body is actually very simple but requires a degree of mindfulness. Mindfulness means to be able to be fully aware and conscious in the present moment without judgement. And although that may sound easy on paper, the reality is that many of us really struggle with mindfulness due to the busy nature of our lives and the constant chatter of our minds. To *truly* be mindful takes a lot of brain training and a lot of practice. Buddhist monks dedicate their lives to the practice of mindful meditation for this exact reason. Although you may not be the next Buddha, you might like to try out some simple mindfulness exercises to help familiarise your body with returning to the present moment the next time it gets lost in unnecessary thought.

Mindful Check-In

This is a simple grounding practice called the 5,4,3,2,1 technique. Maybe you have heard of it? It's especially helpful whenever we are feeling panicked or stressed. This exercise acts as not only a useful distraction from your fear but also prompts you to get back into the present moment and away from your feelings of unsafety via accessing your bodily senses. Once you're in your body, you can focus on slowing your breath down, and you might then find it easier for rational thoughts to come through.

1. Name 5 things you can see. Say them out loud.
2. Name 4 things you can touch around you. Physically touch those things as you acknowledge them and try to become aware of their texture and temperature.
3. Name 3 things you can hear. This could be any external sound.
4. Name 2 things you can smell. You may need to take a brief walk around to find certain things with a scent.
5. Name 1 thing you can taste. This could be a residual taste in your mouth, or you could actively eat or drink something, acknowledging the flavour and sensations in your mouth.

Once you've completed the exercise, check in with your body and nervous system as to how you feel. Perhaps rate the intensity of the panic or stress from before compared to now.

I can't speak about safety without speaking about how the nervous system functions, the vagal nerve, and our breath, so without further ado, are you ready for a lesson in human biology?

Our nervous system (and its ability to respond to stress) is designed to keep us safe and is very much needed for our survival.

> **The practice of self-compassion looks like treating yourself how you would treat the person you love the most in your life.**

Without it, I wouldn't be sitting here writing this book, and you wouldn't be here reading it. It's necessary and incredibly useful. It's our nervous system that allows us to quickly swerve away from incoming traffic, or that gives us the energy and drive required to win a race. Understanding how your nervous system works and the importance between your nervous system, your body, and your thinking brain is crucial because it helps you understand how to find balance. It also helps explain why some of us feel more reactive to seemingly small things than others.

To better know and understand how your nervous system works in relation to trauma and toxic stress, we're going to focus on your autonomic nervous system, which I like to think of as your *automatic* nervous system. This system comprises two primary subsystems known as your sympathetic and parasympathetic nervous systems.

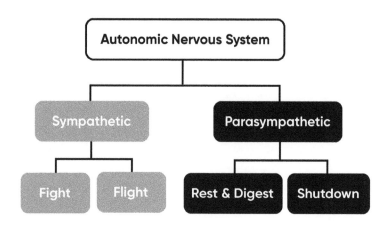

You may have heard of the terms *fight or flight* and *rest and digest* to explain how these systems work. These phrases refer to your sympathetic nervous system and your parasympathetic nervous system, respectively. The sympathetic response activates us, and the parasympathetic relaxes us. We also have what is known as the *freeze response* (also associated with the parasympathetic nervous system), which is the most primitive part of our autonomic nervous system and causes us to freeze like a deer in headlights or to eventually shut down completely when faced with a danger or threat we feel we cannot flee or fight our way out of. Think about a lizard who goes into shock, loses its tail, and freezes to pretend to the predator that it's dead. This form of self-preservation resides within all of us, too.

These three aspects of our nervous system are affected and impacted by something called the vagus nerve, which is one of the most fascinating nerves in the body. In Latin, the word *vagus* means "to wander." The vagus nerve literally translates to "the wandering nerve" as it runs from the 10th cranial nerve in your brain stem and wanders all the way down the length of your torso, having a touchpoint with all your major bodily systems and organs, inclusive of your circulatory system, respiratory system, digestive system, and detoxification system, ending at your large intestine. Pretty wild, right? It literally influences *all* these areas. Its primary function is to send messages to the brain about the state of the body and nervous systems, and to bring the body back into regulation or baseline after moments of stress.

The Vagus Nerve

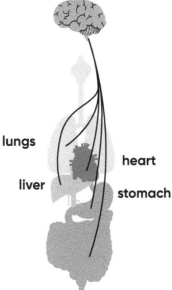

lungs

heart

liver

stomach

So, what does this have to do with the embodiment of safety? Well, a lot.

When we have not recovered from trauma and/or find ourselves in a state of ongoing toxic stress, our vagal nerve does not get the chance to return our body back to that "safe and social" state (a term coined by Stephen Porges, who is the founder of Polyvagal Theory). The longer it remains in a state of dysregulation the more it loses its "vagal tone", which means it becomes unable to properly regulate you and return your nervous system to a state of calm. Our new baseline, therefore, becomes one of either extreme reactivity or extreme wipe-out because our nervous system is stuck in either mode. Being stuck in fight-or-flight mode looks like being completely wired and hyper-aroused, which can come in the following forms: insomnia, anxiety, over-thinking, nervousness, irritability, and hypertension. Alternatively, freeze mode places us in a zombie-like state that is often reflected by a sense of hopelessness, purposelessness, extreme lethargy, depression, and self-sabotaging behaviour. Basically, the state of our nervous system affects our mood, thoughts, and behaviours.

If we are traumatised and stuck in one of these modes of survival, the brain will consistently think it's in a state of danger (even if there is no danger around us), and therefore our behaviours and thoughts will mimic that.

Please don't think that your stress response is faulty, either. As I mentioned earlier, it's very much needed to keep you alive and safe. Without a stress response, you wouldn't be alive. It's also important to note here that a healthy nervous system is not one that is always calm but rather one that is adaptable and resilient, meaning it is able to recover from stressors in a healthy way. It's *such a primal part* of who we are, but when we couple it with the more modern aspects of life and the evolution of our brain development (such as our imagination), it can mistake safety cues for cues of danger and can get stuck responding to memories from our past as if they were still happening in real time. Additionally, if we weren't able to soothe ourselves when our trauma occurred, or if we never learned self-soothing techniques, our body never gets the opportunity to fully process the energetic load of stress. Meaning it gets stuck in our system in the form of implicit memory.

From here it becomes a vicious cycle between brain and body. The nervous system is stuck in its state of hyper- or hypo- arousal so it keeps telling the brain that it's in danger, and then the brain develops thoughts and actively seeks out evidence (confirmation bias) that confirms it is in danger (even when it's not) and these thoughts trap the nervous system in a state of stress. And it keeps going around and around. Exhausting, right?

An example I often use in my therapy sessions to explain this is to imagine a dog crossing the road. The dog goes to cross the road and almost gets hit by a car. Luckily, its sympathetic response kicks in, which stimulates the oxygen, glucose, energy, and focus the dog requires to run to safety and avoid getting hit. The *exact* same thing happens to us from a nervous system perspective. The only difference is that the dog will take a shorter amount of time to recover from the shock, possibly through pacing, panting, or seeking temporary shelter to allow its body to calm down. Then it will get on with its day and continue sniffing trees and rubbish bins. For humans, however, it can be a very different experience. If a person doesn't know how to self-soothe, they won't know how to engage with their breath to calm themselves, or they won't think to shake off the excess energy from fear (which works very well!). Our incredible yet sometimes fickle brain will go on a storytelling tangent about what *could* have happened if the car *did* hit us. Remember that trauma is all about the *meaning* we attach to things. Sometimes these meanings are totally unnecessary thought patterns, but we do it nonetheless as a protective mechanism.

What was that guy thinking driving like that?

Imagine if he did hit me? Oh my gosh, which hospital would I go to? They are all so far away! That makes me feel so anxious.

I wonder if anyone would rescue me if I did get hit. Would my family even care? As you can imagine, such thinking will keep our nervous system activated for way longer than it needs to be. This is why it's so important to learn how everything is interconnected: how our nervous system affects our brain, how our brain affects our nervous system, and how both of these aspects influence our physical body and our thoughts. Trauma is held within us on so many different levels and in so many different ways. It's up to us to learn how to find a sense of safety again, to return to the present moment and regain clarity.

One of the reasons I take a holistic approach with my clients and always integrate both cognitive and somatic practices is because healing trauma requires us to tend to both aspects. It's not *just* the mind that is affected. Trauma is also held within the body since it's where our nervous system lives. And to heal from trauma, the body and the nervous system *must feel safe in order to stop the mind from spiralling.* One of the quickest and most accessible ways to find this inner sense of safety is through your breath.

The breath is possibly one of the simplest yet most overlooked tools we have available to us when it comes to healing and embodied safety. And it's literally available to us 24/7 for free. I don't just say it's important because I am a yoga teacher. I say this because the science behind the breath and how it can bring the body back into presence and safety quicker than any other technique I know is pure magic.

Our breath changes depending on our nervous system response. If we are calm, the breath is slow and steady, and if we are stressed, the breath is short and sharp. It moves this way because when we are stressed, the body needs the oxygen to move to specific parts of the body. The act of hyperventilation keeps our nervous system in an active state of arousal, helping us remain alert to danger. This is what happens when we find ourselves stuck in a trauma response, encountering a stressful moment at work, or simply thinking about something stressful. Our breath changes to support us. Your body is always trying to keep you safe.

The great thing about the breath is that it is one of the only systems we have which is both automatic and controllable. If we pay attention to it, we can manipulate it and change it. This is great news when it comes to regulating the nervous system. It only takes a tiny dose of mindfulness to check in with your body to gauge exactly what's happening. From there it takes conscious attention to shift the quality of the breath, to move you from a state of chaos to a state of calm.

Physiologically speaking, the way the breath moves is obviously governed by the physical movement of the lungs, diaphragm, and rib cage, and the entirety of the respiratory system. Remember how the vagal nerve has a touchpoint to all our major organs and systems? And how it impacts the stress response? Well, one aspect of the breath, and perhaps the only thing you really need to know for now, is that when the diaphragm rises (which happens when we take a proper exhale), it stimulates the vagal nerve positively. It helps "tone" it. When we breathe out, the vagal nerve sends a message to the brain telling us to engage with our parasympathetic response and to calm down. When you think about it logically or from a primal standpoint, it also makes sense. If you have time to exhale fully and slowly, then it must mean that you are safe and that there isn't anything around causing you harm.

Mindful Check-In

Box breathing, also known as square breathing, is a simple yet powerful technique to regulate the nervous system and promote calmness. It involves equalising the lengths of the inhales, exhales, and pauses between, forming a square pattern, hence the name.

1. Find a comfortable seated position, or lie down if you prefer.

2. Close your eyes gently and take a moment to connect with your breath.
3. Inhale slowly and deeply through your nose for a count of four seconds, feeling your abdomen rise as you fill your lungs with air.
4. Hold your breath at the top of your inhale for another count of four seconds, allowing the air to settle within you.
5. Exhale slowly and completely through your mouth for four seconds, feeling your abdomen fall as you release the air from your lungs.
6. At the bottom of your exhale, pause for another count of four seconds before beginning the next cycle.

Repeat this process for several minutes, focusing on the rhythm of your breath and the sensations it creates in your body. If you'd like to, you can extend the breath pattern to 6, 7, or even 8 seconds.

After completing your box breathing session, take a moment to check in with yourself. Notice any changes in your body, mind, and emotions. Pay attention to how you feel compared to before you started the practice. Did you experience a sense of calmness or relaxation? Did any tension or stress dissipate? Allow yourself to witness the impact of the breath, especially the longer exhales.

This was a long explanation of safety, but I want you to be fully aware of how important it is to feel safe within yourself in order to be self-compassionate. When we feel safe, we feel more open to vulnerability because we trust ourselves. We know and have the tools to regulate ourselves, which brings a sense of greater resilience and courage. And when we are more vulnerable, we have greater access to the parts of us that require healing. Trusting in this process and in your ability to soothe is crucial, especially if you grew up in an environment or around caregivers who did not teach you how to do this. The ability to self-soothe is a learned behaviour, meaning that children require adults to help them learn emotional safety and security by first being the safe/secure place for them. Children then slowly learn how to self-soothe as a result. If this wasn't your experience in childhood, don't worry. You can still teach it to yourself now. Alternatively, working with a therapist or trauma-informed practitioner can also help you learn this skill through various techniques and practices but also simply through being your personal co-regulator. They become the safe space you never had, and by being in session with them, you learn how to do it for yourself.

The final framework or theory I want to touch on when it comes to self-compassion is thanks to psychologist, author, and Buddhist meditation teacher, Tara Brach. Tara developed an easy-to-remember acronym called RAIN, which can be done as a meditation practice, a reflection journaling practice, or an in-the-moment practice when you feel stuck in the pits of self-criticism. I have summarised her RAIN model, but you can learn more by researching Tara's work.

R–Recognise what's going on

Recognising involves consciously acknowledging the thoughts, emotions, and behaviours that are present within you at any given moment. This can be as simple as silently noting what you are currently aware of.

A–Allow the experience to be there, just as it is

Allowing entails letting the thoughts, emotions, or sensations you've recognised simply exist without attempting to alter or avoid them. For instance, if you recognise fear, you might accept it by mentally affirming, *It's okay*, or *This is valid*. Acceptance creates a space that allows for deeper awareness and understanding.

I–Investigate with interest and care

To investigate, tap into your innate curiosity and direct a more focused attention to your present experience. You might ask yourself questions such as: *What is most prominent in my awareness? How does this manifest in my body? What beliefs are associated with this experience?*

Regardless of the inquiry, investigating is most transformative when you shift your attention away from conceptualising and focus on the felt sense in your body.

N–Nurture with self-compassion

Self-compassion arises when you acknowledge your own suffering and actively nurture your inner well-being. Begin by identifying what the wounded or frightened part of yourself needs most, then offer a gesture of kindness to address this need.

Experiment with various acts of self-care, such as offering words of reassurance or forgiveness. Additionally, consider gentle physical gestures like placing a hand over your heart or envisioning yourself bathed in warm, loving light.

If extending love to yourself feels challenging, visualise the love and support of a caring figure—whether spiritual, familial, or a friend—flowing into you. This practice of nurturing self-compassion can bring comfort, softness, and an open heart to your inner world.

As I shared at the start of this lesson, teaching compassion is at the heart of what I do, and I truly believe that self-acceptance is nearly impossible without the ability to cultivate compassion. I hope this lesson has ignited your own curiosity into what it means to be compassionate, and perhaps the journal questions here can help show you how you could start implementing more of it into your daily life.

Journal Questions

* How do I respond to my own perceived flaws and inadequacies?
* How often do I blame myself for things that go wrong around me?
* What thoughts come to me about myself when I am in emotional discomfort? Are these thoughts useful to me or not useful?
* Do I treat myself and my setbacks the same way I would treat my best friend who was going through the same thing? If not, why not? What's the difference?
* How could I be more curious and open toward my discomfort? What could this look like in action?
* If I think of something right now that I often criticise myself for, what words of compassion could I offer to myself?

Lesson 11

Acceptance and Forgiveness

Think of compassion as the gateway to radical acceptance. It gives us the tools and perspective to become less rigid and biased about the rules, "should" statements, and boxes in which we place ourselves (and others). We stop taking everything so personally, we stop trying to control the uncontrollable, we start to find spaciousness to live our lives fully. Acceptance has profoundly transformed my life. As you know by now, I used to struggle immensely with acknowledging my internal wounds and feelings of shame. Instead of facing them head-on, I expended tremendous energy attempting to conceal them through perfectionistic behaviours, people-pleasing, and wearing a facade of always being "fine." However, the more I resisted these aspects of myself, the heavier the burden became. It wasn't until I embraced acceptance and allowed myself to acknowledge these parts of me without judgement that I experienced a remarkable shift. A weight lifted off my shoulders, granting me the freedom to authentically be myself. Embracing acceptance opened up space for genuine self-expression and meaningful connections with both myself and others. By accepting my vulnerabilities and imperfections, I discovered a new sense of liberation and authenticity that continues to enrich every aspect of my life.

Acceptance doesn't mean you aren't an agent for change or forward motion, but rather that you are a realist. You tackle things in the here and now rather than fixating on the past or an idea of the future. Acceptance says, *Okay, so this is how it is. I see it and acknowledge it. Now, what do I want to do about it?* Without acceptance, it is very difficult to change or to realise that change is even an option.

The opposite of acceptance would be resistance, denial, and avoidance. When we sit with these feelings, we often feel constricted, heavy, angry, resentful, unforgiving, and narrow-minded. We get nowhere fast by resisting life, yet so many of us prefer to stay in this state because we believe that accepting things will make everything more painful. The cost to us when we resist life takes a drastic toll emotionally, energetically, and physically.

Sometimes acceptance results in temporary pain as we acknowledge the reality of a situation. So, it's no surprise that resisting that pain for as long as possible might seem like the better option. Eventually, however, it always catches up to us. For me, the practice of acceptance is one of the hardest mindsets to master. I'm definitely still working on it!

When we consider acceptance via the lens of a society that conditions us to feel shame our thoughts can sound like:

Why would I accept something that is flawed?

How can I just sit back and accept that I am broken? Or faulty? Or not good enough? If I accept myself as I am surely no one will love me.

It can feel really hard to truly accept ourselves because, sadly, many of us feel as though the people who should have really truly accepted us (our caregivers) did not. So, how can we? In the same way that we don't learn how to regulate our emotions if our parents also didn't know how, we don't learn how to accept ourselves if our belief is that no one ever has, or if acceptance was never demonstrated to us in the first place. We simply don't know *how* to do it. Additionally, we may find it hard to accept ourselves and all our emotions because society and our upbringing tell us that there are "good" and "bad" emotions. And so, whenever we feel sadness, for example, we resist it or avoid it out of shame rather than accept it as a normal human response.

Being able to effectively process our emotions helps us with the normalisation of them and provides us with the ability to feel more in control of ourselves and resilient to life's ups and downs. So, how does one properly feel our feelings? You may have heard of the term "to hold space." It's a common phrase used by healers, therapists, coaches, and yoga teachers, and it simply means to create a safe physical and energetic space for a person to express themselves fully with no judgement. Therapists are trained in this practice so they can help others feel at ease sharing their thoughts, emotions, and memories and, as a result, teach them how to be more accepting of themselves. But it can also (and perhaps more importantly) help us the most if we can learn to do it introspectively.

So again, the definition of holding space is:

To create a safe physical and energetic space for a person to express themselves fully with no judgement.

The opposite of this would be to criticise them ("Ugh, how embarrassing, you're crying again"), or to minimise their experience through something like toxic positivity ("Chin up! You'll be alright").

Neither of these tactics work as they only feed the belief that the person and their emotion, thought, or expression is "bad." If we realise that our emotions are not who we are but rather just something we feel, we stop fearing the emotions or letting them define our identity. They are quite literally just chemical reactions in your body. That's it. In fact, there is a "90 second rule" about emotions coined by neuroanatomist and author Dr Jill Bolte Taylor.

She states that:

"When a person has a reaction to something in their environment, there's a 90 second chemical process that happens in the body; after that, any remaining emotional response is just the person choosing to stay in that emotional loop. Something happens in the external world and chemicals are flushed through your body which puts it on full alert. For those chemicals to totally flush out of the body takes less than 90 seconds. This means that for 90 seconds you can watch the process happening, you can feel it happening, and then you can watch it go away. After that, if you continue to feel fear, anger, and so on, you need to look at the thoughts that you're thinking that are re-stimulating the circuitry that is resulting in you having this physiological response over and over again."

Fascinating, right? To know that our emotions can come and go but it's our thoughts, memories, and reactions to them that keep them lingering for longer. If we resist what we feel, it gets bigger. If we can accept it knowing that it too shall pass, it does.

The same process applies with the thousands and thousands of thoughts we have each day. We must first accept that we are humans who have thoughts. We must then accept that not all our thoughts are true, helpful, or necessary and that our thoughts do not define us in any way. And third, we must learn to respond to our thoughts in a way that acknowledges them but doesn't give them more meaning than required. Meditation helps a lot with this. Instead of allowing our thoughts to dictate our emotions and behaviours, we can learn to accept that they are there and to simply observe them for what they are—just thoughts. Something that really helps with this process of acceptance is by saying to yourself, *I'm having the thought that...* before any of your confronting or challenging thoughts and notice how that simple phrase gives you distance and less reactivity to it. So, instead of saying, *I am a bad person*, you can say, *I am having the* thought *that I am a bad person*. Accept that it's just a thought. You are not your thoughts. You are the person who has thoughts. There is a difference. Try it now with a few of your critical thoughts and see what happens.

Learning how to hold space for yourself means becoming very familiar with your mental and emotional landscape and applying all aspects of self-compassion to them. Accepting them for what they are rather than resisting, avoiding, or denying them. Because to be emotional or have critical thoughts, or thoughts which aren't true is, once again, a normal part of the human experience. In Buddhism they often refer to this ability to be the observer of oneself as being a "loving witness". To view yourself through the lens of love and kindness and compassion as you watch your human experience unfold. The more we can learn to zoom out of ourselves, the more we start to see ourselves from a very different perspective. Objectivity is a key element when it comes to being more accepting of ourselves and others.

The other reason why many of us fear acceptance is because it can give us a feeling of powerlessness or lack of control. If I accept things for what they are (which might mean accepting something I don't want or like), then I might make it mean that everything will *always* be bad and difficult and that I will never recover from it. I become scared of the possibility of spiralling out of control. Lack of control evokes a similar feeling to vulnerability in the sense that it exposes us to the risk of being hurt. In reality, it only acts as a risk if

> To hold space is to create a safe physical and energetic space for a person to express themselves fully with no judgement.

we let it be a risk. The reason we see it as risky is because we don't *trust* in our ability to face our reality. We are scared of how we will react and that we don't have the tools to support us.

If you think about it logically, however, resisting your reality or avoiding your life is more in line with you being *out* of control. Because if you truly felt *in* control you'd be able to face it head-on. In short, if you don't trust yourself, you'll always fear the path of acceptance. Radical acceptance is testament to someone who is fully empowered, fully trusting of their emotional regulation, fully aware of their story and the limitations of their mind, and truly self-compassionate. This entire book is a guide toward greater self-acceptance. It's all these things that allow you to be authentically you and fully present in your life.

Acceptance of ourselves and of our thoughts and emotions is not where acceptance ends. Acceptance applies both to self as well as to others and the world at large. We cannot control what other people have done, we cannot control everything that happens around us, and we can't get angry every time someone doesn't see things from the same perspective as we do. We need to learn to accept that not everything is the way we want it to be or the way we think it should be. That's just life. The quicker we accept it, the more at peace we will be and, ironically, the more in control we will feel.

We want to control everything because it makes us feel safe. More specifically, it makes the ego feel safe, as it keeps you within the confines of the stories and beliefs of your mind. But a huge part of the problem is that we are always seeking to control the uncontrollable, namely the things outside ourselves. If I spend my life trying to micromanage my outside world, I will forever be disappointed and disheartened. It's like the pursuit of perfection: It's a downward spiral because perfect doesn't exist. Nor does a world where everything goes the way you want it to. One of the greatest takeaways in my life has been the acceptance of suffering as a normal part of the human experience. It's normal to have shitty days, it's normal to get triggered sometimes, even if you are actively doing the work. It's normal that people will let you down, it's normal to feel uncomfortable emotions such as sadness and anger and frustration, it's normal that not everyone will like you just as you don't like everyone. Accept that this is all *normal*. Without these experiences, without pain and suffering and difficulty and emotional lows, you wouldn't even know what joy or happiness or comfort felt like. Life would be pretty bland.

Like right now. Can you accept that you hold some feelings of shame around certain aspects of who you are and that it is due to the consequences of your life experiences and the stories you have told yourself? Remember that shame grows in secrecy. So just speak it out loud. Accept it. "I feel ashamed of myself in this way…" It's okay. I have never met anyone who doesn't feel ashamed of some aspect of who they are. Once again, let's normalise it; let's not make it wrong. Let's accept it as a current reality so we can move forward.

If the battle of not being good enough gets louder the more I resist my authenticity, then doesn't it make sense that the antidote would be to accept myself wholeheartedly as an imperfectly normal, whole, and complex human being?

Whenever I speak about the acceptance process with my clients, especially when we are talking about other people, one of the most common questions is:

"But how can I accept bad behaviour?"

In other words, how can I let go or forgive someone or myself for wrongdoing or betrayal? Surely, they/I must be punished for the rest of their/my lives/life?

Forgiveness and acceptance go hand in hand and are crucial in the overcoming of shame and perfectionistic thinking. They are one and the same. Once you can understand this, you'll realise that forgiveness has very little to do with the other person or the event and a hell of a lot more to do with you and your innate sense of freedom. Forgiveness is a portal toward relief. A weight off your shoulders.

Self-Reflection

＊ What does holding a grudge feel like to you?
＊ What emotions arise when you think of something or someone whom you cannot yet forgive?
＊ Where do you experience this in your body? Are the sensations pleasant or unpleasant?
＊ What is the purpose of holding on?
＊ What does holding on give you?
＊ What does it cost you?

These questions will apply regardless of whether you are forgiving yourself or another person. The most important part is the realisation that holding on to a grudge or resentment costs you time, energy, physical pain, and a lack of energetic and emotional freedom. It's a huge weight to carry. One of my favourite Buddhist quotes on the topic says that "holding on to anger is like grasping a hot coal with the intention of throwing it at someone else; you are the one who gets burned."

Many people don't want to forgive because their belief is that if they forgive or accept, it means it makes the wrongdoing right. Or that what happened will happen again. As I said previously, though, forgiveness is more about you than about them. You can forgive someone and not tell them you have forgiven them. You can forgive someone and choose to still not have them in your life because it is unsafe. Forgiveness isn't about letting someone hurt you again or hurting yourself again. It's about the acceptance that *something* happened that you didn't like or didn't make you feel good. It's acceptance that we cannot change the past. That people (including you) are human and make mistakes or have shortcomings because of what they did not know at the time or have not yet healed within themselves. I truly believe that we can only operate in this life to the degree that we have healed and understood our own stories.

When I was a teenager I used to say to my mother, "I love him because he is my father, but I dislike who he is as a person." For so many years of my life I held anger toward my father. Anger, confusion, fear, immense hurt, sadness, and heartbreak. It felt heavy, constricting, tight, and never-ending. It took so much of my energy, and I honestly believe it's one of the main reasons why as a child I was so sickly, always having issues with migraines and inflamed tonsils. My head and my throat were completely overworked and out of whack. The manifestation of my discomfort into my physiology was real. And the thing is that as a child and even up until my early twenties, I didn't know enough about all of this to forgive him. So, I held on to these feelings and carried it all with me.

It wasn't until I started doing therapy when I was about nineteen that I realised the weight of what I was holding. I couldn't speak about my father without crying. I remember sitting in the therapy room and just crying for the first hour, and then my session was up. I had not yet accepted my emotions, and that was the first time I properly just sat with them and allowed them to surface. It was a profound shifting point. I was able to witness the sadness, the grief, the shame, the hope, the fears, the longing, the anger... all of it. I realised as I watched myself and worked through my own patterns and conditioning that my dad *also* had patterns and reasons as to why he was the way he was. And so I applied (without realising it) many of the steps of compassion to better understanding my father and also the nature of our relationship and how it evolved over time. I examined both him and myself with nonjudgemental curiosity, and I found out more about his own childhood and his own wounds. I understood that he was hurting so much, too, and that, unfortunately, I was in the firing line of his pain. Now this doesn't mean that I'm excusing bad behaviour. Nor that I am saying it's OK to shame or bully your children. But it meant that I could see him as *human* rather than placing him in a box of expectation of how a perfect father "should" be. And when I could see him as human, I could accept him. And in my heart I could forgive him. Despite our difficult relationship, I know and have always known that he loves me and that he's proud of me and that he would do anything and everything for me. I also know that I was a trigger for him and how that resulted in many of our conflicts.

I made a choice to keep my father in my life because, in the end, my understanding of him and my love and compassion for him outweighed any anger or sadness. The more I learned about my own emotions and how to create my own energetic and physical boundaries (more on that in the next lesson), the safer I felt around him. I could see all the ways he *did* love me, and all the things he *did* do for me and our family, and how hard he tried and how much of himself he gave to provide us with the quality of life we had. I also could feel and have empathy for how much pressure he was under trying to provide for us, how stressful his job was, how he did not have the tools for self-regulation, how he already held his own guilt about his actions. Guilt is such a hard emotion to navigate; I didn't need to make that worse for him.

I don't know if I've ever explicitly told my father that I forgive him. It was more a me thing than a him thing. But I know he could feel that I had let go of a lot of my pain in the way I responded to him and moved toward him rather than away from him. And I think that him sensing a change in me helped him let go of some of his own pain, too. As he's gotten older, he has become so much softer, so much more open, so much more accepting of his own shortcomings. He's a better listener; he's not angry anymore. He even asked me to teach him yoga not long ago, and it was one of the best messages I received all year! I know that he is healing, too, in his own unique way. I cherish our moments together now because I feel I missed out on such moments with him in childhood. I cherish watching him be a grandfather to my son, and I am so proud of us and how far we have come. When I was eight and a half months pregnant my father had a heart attack. I was sitting at my desk and got a message on my phone from my mom that said, "we are at the hospital—dad had a heart attack last night." My heart dropped into my chest and I wanted to throw up. The thought of him not meeting my baby, all the emotions from my past, my deep love for him... It all came rushing through me like a tidal wave. Luckily after surgery he was OK. His health has never been his strong point. But it was a moment in my life where I was incredibly thankful for all the work I had done on myself and how happy I was that I made the decision to let go of any anger or pain toward him.

I share my story not to make you feel like you have to keep people in your life who have betrayed you or wronged you, but just to see what one aspect of forgiveness can look like. As a therapist I obviously work a lot with the ruptures of attachment between adult children and their parents. Some of my clients find acceptance and choose to cultivate a relationship with boundaries, and others find acceptance but choose to not have that person in their life. There is no wrong or right. Forgiveness is just about you letting go of the pain you hold because you realise that holding on is more of a punishment to *you* than it is to anyone else.

When it comes to self-forgiveness, it's the same deal. We often hold ourselves to the expectations and standards of who we are now and what we know now, when much of what we did in our past was done with much less awareness, emotional maturity, and self-compassion. Don't judge yourself and punish yourself for what you did not know back then. Instead, put yourself in the shoes of who you *were* then and what was going on for you, and become compassionate about the life experiences and beliefs you once held. Understand that that version of you probably did or said what she did or said because it was an understandable thing to do considering everything. And that's okay. Shame has no place here. Can you simply make some space for that truth? How could you offer some compassionate validation to your experience? What words of wisdom will help you realise that punishing yourself isn't the easiest path ahead of you?

A simple practice I like to offer my clients to experiment with is the Hawaiian teaching of the Ho'oponopono prayer, which roughly translates to "bringing things back into balance". It's a mantra for the self as well as for others. It's forged around love, gratitude, and forgiveness. The practice itself involves sitting quietly in meditation and repeating the following words to yourself:

"I'm sorry. Please forgive me. Thank you. I love you."

As you say this mantra repeatedly, observe the waves of relief and warmth that come into your heart space, your shoulders, and the rest of your being. Notice who or what comes to mind as you repeat the lines, and see if you can make each word more and more meaningful with every repetition. It's a simple yet profound practice to do daily, if possible.

Journal Questions

* Where in my life do I experience resistance?
* What is the consequence of resistance for me emotionally and physically?
* What biases or judgements do I have toward being more accepting?
* Do I hold any grudges toward myself or others? If so, what are they, and why do they exist?
* What biases or judgements do I hold about forgiveness?
* If there are aspects of my past that I am struggling with, what words of acceptance and forgiveness could I offer myself? Is it fair to judge myself *then* based on who I am and what I know *now*?

Lesson 12

Cultivating Self-Respect and Creating Boundaries

If we feel not good enough, then chances are we are treating ourselves accordingly. And remember, the brain needs repetition—be it words, action, or otherwise—to rewire its neural pathways.

Self-respect comes from the way we treat ourselves. By treating ourselves well, others will also treat us well because we are setting the standard for what we deserve.

In other words, *how you respect yourself is how you teach others to respect you.*

Building self-respect comes from treating yourself like you are *worthy* of it. It's about the small, everyday practices and actions which, over time, build esteem, confidence, trust, and a more positive attitude toward life. If we respect ourselves, trust ourselves, and carry ourselves with an energy of worthiness, what we receive will be attuned to our mindset. Because our thoughts create our actions, remember? If you change your mindset, you will naturally shift your actions, and the shift in actions will create choices, open doorways, or provoke decision-making, which would not have otherwise happened if you remained in the mindset of unworthiness, shame, and not-good-enoughness.

One of the key aspects of cultivating self-respect is setting clear boundaries: boundaries with yourself and others. And that's what this lesson is all about.

When we feel unworthy, often we will hold boundaries that are either too rigid (i.e., never letting anyone in for fear of being hurt, judged, or betrayed) or too porous (i.e., not knowing how to say no and spending our life people-pleasing). The shame associated

> By treating ourselves well, others will also treat us well because we are setting the standard for what we deserve.

with our story of not being good enough leaves us in a state of fear regardless of how we look at it. We also tend to cross boundaries with ourselves when we operate from this place of not enoughness, which results in self-sabotaging behaviour and a continuous breaking of promises to ourselves, further perpetuating our guilt, remorse, self-pity, and shame.

A boundary is essentially a space of safety that you operate within. It's a deep knowledge of your values and what makes your life feel *meaningful*. You must then translate that into what it would look like—or not look like—in real-life experiences.

For example, if you value communication because it makes you feel seen, heard, and understood, then it would make your life feel *meaningful* to have friendships and relationships where communication is easy, open, and honest. On the flip side, a boundary-crossing for you might be engaging in a relationship with someone who doesn't communicate, holds things back, gaslights you, or can't express how they feel. A personal boundary-cross for you could be not using your voice and expressing your perspective when you feel called to. Both boundary-crossings would leave you feeling deflated, uneasy, resentful, and stressed, and as a result, life would feel more meaningless.

A great way to help you implement healthy boundaries into your life is to use the following four steps:

Step 1: Know Your Values

This part often gets missed. Clients often say to me, "But how am I supposed to just *know* what my boundaries are?" and they are right. It's super hard to just reel off your boundaries if you don't know where they stem from or how they make you feel when they are crossed. The thing about boundaries, as I mentioned earlier, is that they are interlinked with your values. And your values are what give your life a sense of purpose. If you live in accordance with your values, you will feel pretty damn good. And if you don't, you won't. It's simple. So, to know your boundaries you *must* know your values.

Exercise
KNOWING YOUR VALUES

1. When in your life have you felt totally in alignment and in flow? What was happening around you and for you?
2. When observing other people, who tends to inspire you? What qualities do they have, or what are they doing with their lives?
3. When did your mind and body feel the most energetic, open, and healthy? How were you treating it? What lifestyle were you leading?
4. How would you like your partner/best friend to describe you if they were talking to someone else?
5. Imagine sitting with your grandchildren one day and describing to them how your life has been/

felt so far. What words would you want to use?

6. What is something you talk about doing but never get around to?

7. What do you feel is missing from your life?

8. What advice would you give to your 16-year-old self?

In reviewing the answers to these questions, what will become evident for you are certain words, actions, or things that hold meaning. For example, a few of my personal values include communication, honesty, trust, compassion, education, wholesome food, cooking, family togetherness, presence, cleanliness, homeliness, structure, and alone time.

Step 2: Write down what your values would look like in action

For this part of the process, you want to determine what your values would look like in action both toward yourself and from others. Honouring your *own* boundaries and living up to your *own* values is arguably much more important than someone else doing it. After all, you're the one who has to live with you 24/7, and if you're constantly betraying yourself, you're not going to feel very good.

Create two columns and write down what these values would look like in real-life scenarios. I've given an example of my own to help you, and I invite you to do the same in your own journal.

	What I need from Self	What I need from Others
Communication	Journaling, seeing my therapist regularly, meditation, being open with people I trust and not holding myself back from sharing my voice.	Active listening, being present with me whilst I am communicating, showing interest in what I am saying, not speaking over me, not yelling at me, not gaslighting me, not staring at their phone while I am speaking.
Honesty	Being honest with others about how I feel or what I want. Asking for help. Not hiding my emotions. Being realistic about my money issues. Not being a hypocrite.	Truthfulness, even if it will hurt me in the short term. Feeling included in my partner's and my close friends' lives. Not being kept in the dark. No secrets. No betrayal.
Structure	I function best when I have a good night's sleep, get up early, move my body, and eat a full breakfast. I am most productive when I utilise my calendar and plan my work, so I don't get overwhelmed. I enjoy knowing what I have ahead of me in a week.	To not change plans last minute. To not have clients who don't show up to therapy or who run late all the time. To have other people come to things on time if they can. I value my time and others a lot, and structure helps me ensure this value is also met.
Alone time	To speak up when I need to be alone rather than putting myself into situations where I feel uncomfortable. To schedule alone time in my week so that I don't exhaust myself.	To respect my need for alone time and not misinterpret it as me being rude.

Step 3: Identify times in the past when your boundaries were crossed

This exercise helps you know what it feels like to have a boundary crossed and gets you thinking about the space of safety in which you'd like to operate.

I usually get my clients to think of at least three to five times when a boundary has been crossed within different areas of their life: career, family, romantic relationship, friendships, and self.

I ask them to identify the following things:

1. What happened.
2. How they reacted.
3. Why they reacted that way (the value or boundary that was compromised).
4. The story they told themselves ("when it happened, it meant to me that...")
5. What they would have liked to have happened instead.

Once again, the invitation is to do the same exercise in relation to your own experiences. Write down as many as come to mind. The more familiar you become with what it feels like to have a boundary crossed, what it meant to you, and what you need in future, the easier it will be for you to communicate your boundaries to others or learn to respect them for yourself.

Remember that the path of reconnection is about understanding ourselves and what we need to feel safe, worthy, and present.

The more self-inquiry you do, the more confident you will become at expressing yourself and navigating your life with ease.

Step 4: Learn how to communicate your boundaries to yourself and others

Communication is usually the hardest part. So many people struggle with communication, but if you don't express your expectations or needs, how are you supposed to get what you want? People aren't mind readers, and ultimately it's up to us to share how something has made us feel or what we expect out of something.

The reason why communication is so hard, though, is because many of us were not witness to healthy communication as children. Perhaps we did not feel safe to communicate for whatever reason, or perhaps we did not learn how to use our voice in a way that made us feel understood or empowered. We may hold innate beliefs such as *My voice doesn't matter* or *No one listens to me*. For many of my clients there was an expectation of them as children to be seen and not heard, meaning that self-expression may have been ignored, belittled, or resulted in punishment, which understandably results in a fear of communication.

There are five different types of communication style when it comes to how people express themselves. The main styles that will show up in your life will be dependent on the circumstances of your lived experiences (everything we covered in the first part of this book). It's important to understand your communication style to know what you need to do to make it more healthy or assertive, but also to understand other people's communication styles.

This helps you better identify how to approach them in a way that doesn't feel threatening or triggering for them. Trust me when I say that refining the way you communicate and learning how to navigate other people's styles will result in much less conflict and much more clarity for everyone involved.

Before we jump into how to express your boundaries to another person, I feel it's important to share what the five communication styles are.

1. Aggressive

An aggressive communicator is focused on their own needs and sees communication as a battle to be won. It's likely that this person grew up in an environment where they had to be loud to be heard and that aggression was a normal means of expression within the childhood environment. An aggressive communicator is highly reactive and will be quick to take offence to everything and anything being said. Because they fight to win, they don't really listen to understand, let alone listen at all. It's common for this type of communicator to use a loud tone of voice, to speak over the other person, to use foul language, to name-call, and to express their aggression through physical acts (such as slamming doors or throwing things). When it comes to boundaries, an aggressive communicator usually has very rigid boundaries, hence their opinion that it's "my way or the highway."

If you resonate as an aggressive communicator, doing a lot of self-inquiry work will be useful in understanding the stories you tell yourself about being "under attack." The rise to aggressiveness says that there is an assumption that other people are out to get you or hurt you. The aggression is merely a defence mechanism in the extreme. It's important to learn to listen properly and to hear what is being said rather than only hearing the parts that can turn into an attack on your character.

If you are dealing with an aggressive communicator, it's important to not rise up to meet their aggression as it will only make it worse. Co-regulation is the ability for one person's nervous system to influence another, and this is very powerful when dealing with a person who is in "defence mode." Keep your nervous system calm, seek clarification as to why they are upset, ask them what they need, and if it gets too much, express that it is too much and request a break from the conversation.

2. Passive

The opposite of the aggressive communicator, a passive communicator has no focus on their own needs and is completely focused on the needs of the other person. Driven by a fear of being a disappointment, these people are usually the people-pleasers, the introverts, and those who feel anxious or scared to use their voice. It's highly likely that as a child, they were not encouraged to speak up (better to be seen and not heard), or that they were belittled or punished when they tried to express themselves. They have an inner belief that everyone else matters more than they do, and therefore communication will be very, very difficult for them, even scary. During confrontation they tend to freeze up, to forget what they want to say, to start crying or get overwhelmed, or to apologise for things that are not their fault.

If you resonate as a passive communicator, learning how to feel safe when speaking will be really important. Writing down what you want to say, taking time to understand your thoughts and feelings, and learning how to put them into words will be so useful for you. Even bringing a piece of paper into confrontations to keep you on track will help. The consequence of not speaking up is resentment and a perpetuation of the belief that you are not good enough and that your voice doesn't matter. Taking breaths between sentences, asking for time, and practicing with people you trust first will be super helpful.

If you are dealing with a passive communicator, understand how scary confrontation is for them, and create an energetic space of safety. This might involve not speaking over them, asking them if it's okay to share your opinion once they've finished speaking, gaining clarification on what they have heard, encouraging them to expand on what they are saying, and being patient with their expression (e.g., not rushing them, ending their sentences, or speaking over them).

3. Passive-Aggressive

I like to refer to this person as the smiling assassin. The passive-aggressive communicator is the person whose favourite expression is "I'm fine" whilst very obviously not being fine. You might be nodding your head in agreement with this, as I know many people fall into this category. Sharing similar fears to that of a passive communicator, this person is also scared of confrontation, usually due to punishment, lack of encouragement, or ignorance of their voice as a child. They feel hurt but don't want to engage in the conversation because it's too hard and too difficult to find the words. There is an assumption that all confrontation leads to conflict, so they would rather not say anything at all. Instead, they will demonstrate their emotions through their actions. In other words, when they say "I'm fine" it doesn't align with their avoidant or aggressive behaviour. A passive-aggressive communicator will show they are unhappy or unsettled by ignoring your calls, being short with you, not engaging in plans like they used to, or bitching about you behind your back. When you confront them on these actions, they might deny it's happening, leaving you feeling very confused and stuck as to how to move forward. The main problem with a passive-aggressive person is that they assume people can read their minds and that everyone should just know why they are upset or disgruntled.

If you resonate as a passive-aggressive person, learning that speaking up and sharing your truth is much less painful than holding it all in will be your greatest lesson. A result of this behaviour is deep resentment toward others, loneliness, and oftentimes guilt at the knowing your behaviour isn't appropriate. Similar tools and practices can apply to you as those of passive communicators, along with doing the self-inquiry work on the story that people are out to hurt you. Making assumptions that everyone is out to get you or that people are inconsiderate of you will only heighten your feeling of loneliness and cause you to further avoid people and isolate yourself. Addressing the root cause of this behaviour will be hugely beneficial for you.

If you are dealing with a passive-aggressive communicator, it can be very hard to get them to open up and want to talk in the first place. Learning to read body language and nonverbal communication will be of benefit to determine what their perspective of the situation might be. These people need to feel safe to use their voice, so patience is key. You also need to remind them that they are important and that you genuinely care and want to work things out with them. Becoming curious about their perspective on things and helping them find clarity will be highly useful for both of you.

4. Manipulative

The most difficult communication style of all is the manipulator. They are focused on their own needs and desires rather than the needs and desires of anyone else. Unlike the aggressive communicator, they won't use force to get what they want. Instead, they will cleverly manipulate the other person into giving them what they want without realising it. This skill is quite impressive but very dangerous when used with selfish intent. A manipulative communicator has a good awareness and understanding of what makes others tick. Often, this trait is associated with other narcissistic behaviours. People who are friends with or acquainted with manipulative people will not initially realise what is going on but will soon enough feel used, taken advantage of, or tricked into a false sense of friendship or safety. A manipulative person will use anything that serves them to get what they want. This could involve gaslighting, aggression, sarcasm, guilt-tripping, or even showering the other person with compliments and praise. Interestingly, one of the other places I have worked where people have openly owned being manipulative has been within the drug and alcohol rehab clinic. Understandably, the lies, secrecy, and unpredictable nature that comes with addiction requires a strong degree of manipulation from the addict to maintain relationships during their period of addiction.

If you resonate as a manipulative person, becoming aware of your intentions will help you consider both people within the conversation. Ask yourself where your intentions are coming from and whether the way you are acting is in line with your values and who you want to be. Changing our ways can be hard, so learning and inquiring into where you picked up these behaviours, and why, will assist you in the path of self-realisation. It's hard to admit that we are being selfish, so speaking up or asking for help or forgiveness when appropriate can also be useful, as well as engaging in therapy. Lastly, practicing the art of selflessness will be a beautiful practice for you. Experimenting with doing things for others, acts of charity, and gestures of kindness will shift your manipulative ways.

If you are dealing with a manipulator, it will depend on your ability to see through their manipulative ways as to whether you will find equal ground in communicating with them. Compassionately pointing out what they are doing and asking why they are doing it will force them to self-reflect (even if they don't want to). Sometimes, however, it can be best to work with a mediator or therapist when things get hard. A third party can help minimise manipulation and ensure both parties are seen and heard. And finally, if things just don't or won't change, deciding if you can keep this person in your life will be a choice that might need to be considered.

5. Assertive

The ideal style of communication is an assertive style. Being assertive does not mean being aggressive. It means being direct and honest about what is going on for you. An assertive person has a good understanding of themselves and can articulate what is going on for them with relative ease. They know how to self-regulate and, therefore, confrontation is rarely associated with fear. Even if they experience anxiety beforehand, they know how to get themselves back into the present moment in order to express themselves. They value resolution above all else, which means they are genuinely driven by their own interests and perspectives, as well as the interests and perspectives of others to find a way to move forward. An assertive person is happy to agree to disagree if that's where the conversation goes. They accept that people have different perspectives. They can express themselves and hold space for the other to do the same.

If you resonate as an assertive communicator, then you're on the right path and have obviously been putting in the work to broaden your perspective and develop your innate ability to self-regulate. Sometimes when we get to this space and realise how powerful it is to be able to communicate well, we can get frustrated when others aren't in the same place of self-development. Try to be patient here. People only develop and learn at a pace that is in alignment with their awareness and willingness to do so. Use your skills to be able to meet them where they are, and demonstrate through action what effective communication can look and feel like.

The interesting thing about communication styles is that we might find ourselves to generally be assertive, healthy communicators, but with one specific person or group of people, we shift into a different style. For example, when I was working on my own communication, I felt that over time I became a really good communicator with friends and colleagues, but no matter how hard I tried, I still shifted into this passive style whenever it came to my father or romantic partners. The more assertive I became in every other aspect of my life, the more I realised just how much healing I still had to do when it came to that attachment wound. If that resonates for you, it doesn't mean you are wrong or stupid. It just means there is more healing and attention that needs to go into finding safety within yourself, your beliefs, and with what that other person or people represent. I would say that I am a very assertive communicator now (it's taken me ten plus years to get here), but I would be lying if I told you that I don't *still* get a bit anxious, scared, and stuck if I need to have a confrontational discussion with my father or my husband. It takes a *lot* of self-regulation for me still to breathe my way through the conversation and remind myself that I am no longer a child. If I don't do this, I will very easily regress into my childlike state of being very, very passive. So, the takeaway here is that communication is hard, and that you will sometimes still get triggered, because you are human. It's not going to be perfect every single time. But practice, practice, practice as much as possible. The more you practice, the easier it gets.

Understanding our own communication styles and the communication styles of others is crucial because it directly influences how we articulate and assert our boundaries effectively. When something happens to us that crosses a boundary, it's important to speak to it and express it rather than bottle it up in resentment or blow up about it. It's equally important to set expectations. If you have had a bad experience in the past, then it's up to you to set an expectation based on that experience with any new person in your life if you feel that it could occur again.

When we cross our own boundaries, we still need to recognise what has happened, communicate it with ourselves, and take action to ensure we don't do it again. If we can't do this, we end up breaking our own trust; we are proving to ourselves time and time again that we don't respect ourselves. Self-trust is an essential skill to cultivate when it comes to making changes or growing in new ways. Without it, everything feels much harder and scarier. So, as much as you may want to focus on how others cross your boundaries, the invitation is to always also check in on how you might be crossing your own, too. Arguably that's even more important.

When it comes to other people, knowing how to communicate our feelings in an assertive way is a skill worth cultivating. Before communicating anything with anyone, it's always important to ask them for their time. Presence is needed for effective communication, and we cannot assume that another person is ready to talk about things just because we are. Being caught off-guard with a confrontational discussion can cause reactions or assumptions which are otherwise avoidable. So, always ask for someone's time.

My favourite model for communicating boundaries is as follows:

1. State the facts only

Don't go off on a tangent about how the other person "made you feel" straight away. All the other person will hear if you do this is blame and therefore be quick to get defensive. Facts are not up for debate: A fact is a fact. This should be simply stating exactly what happened as it happened with no room for ifs or buts.

For example:

> "When I saw you at lunch with your ex-girlfriend..."
> "When you turned up twenty-five minutes late to my event..."
> "When I waved to you, and you didn't wave back..."
> "When we went to the party, and I realised that I didn't know anyone but you did..."

2. Express how it made you feel

This is where you get to express the emotion it aroused within you. Emotion is not always something people can understand the origins of, but they can at least resonate with the emotion itself because everyone has experienced common emotions such as sadness, anger, jealousy, excitement, anxiety, fear, embarrassment, etc.

For example:

> "When you turned up twenty-five minutes late to my event, it made me feel sad and confused."

3. Express why it made you feel that way

Here is where your perspective comes in. The story you tell yourself. Knowing all you now know about our differing life experiences, beliefs, and values, you will know that everyone wears a unique lens in how they see the world. This is where you get to share your perspective to help the other person understand where and how the emotion has arisen.

For example:

> "When you turned up twenty-five minutes late to my event, it made me feel sad and confused. I was telling myself that you didn't care about this event and that I am not important to you."

4. What did it remind you of (if anything)?

If you really feel comfortable with the person you are communicating with and have a good awareness of self, you might like to expand on the story with insight into what it reminded you of.

For example:

> "When you turned up twenty-five minutes late to my event, it made me feel sad and confused. I was telling myself that you didn't care about this event and that I am not important to you. It reminded me so much of how my parents used to forget to pick me up from school or attend my events as a child and it brought up all those emotions."

5. State your request/expectation/boundary

What do you need to help you feel safer in this situation? This is where you state your expectation or boundary in relation to the situation. Bear in mind that your request needs to be realistic in relation to the person you are dealing with/situation you are in. It wouldn't be reasonable, for example, for you to expect your boss to treat you the same way you'd request your intimate partner to treat you.

For example:

> "When you turned up twenty-five minutes late to my event, it made me feel sad and confused. I was telling myself that you didn't care about this event and that I am not important to you. It reminded me so much of how my parents used to forget to pick me up from school or attend my events as a child and brought up all those emotions. What would mean a lot to me in the future is if you would send me a quick message to let me know you are running late and why, so that I know you are still thinking of me and intend to be here."

6. Open the conversation up if necessary

Lastly, and once again if the relationship allows it, it can be useful and respectful to gain clarification that the other person understands or if they have any questions or perspectives they would like to offer. If we can cultivate healthy communication within any form of relationship, it strengthens the relationship and helps us understand more and more about the other person. This, in turn, benefits everyone involved as we start to realise how to safely operate within the bubble of that relationship.

So, you could ask things such as, "Does that make sense?" or "Do you understand where I'm coming from?" or "Is that okay with you?" or "Is there anything you wanted to say to this?"

At the end of the day, practice makes everything easier, and this is especially true when it comes to communication and boundaries. Some people think that boundaries are like an electric fence: reactive, shocking, and oftentimes aggressive and hostile. They don't *need* to be like that, and the only reason they become that way is usually because of a build-up of things left unsaid and a suppression of deep resentment.

Obviously there will be times when *no* is a complete sentence, and you will know when this is appropriate. Most of the time, though, I do believe that it is achievable to navigate our boundaries with kindness, compassion, and respect. I believe that for the most part, boundaries *help* us foster closer and more meaningful relationships rather than being a tool used to push people away. The way we treat and respect ourselves is essentially how we teach others to treat and respect us. A difficult truth to digest is that when a boundary line has been crossed, it is usually because we have *allowed* it. That may sound harsh, but it's true. Unless someone is physically stronger than we are and we are completely incapable of defending ourselves or removing ourselves, a boundary-cross usually happens because we haven't set the expectation in the first place, we haven't reminded them of it, or we haven't had the courage to speak up and set the boundary when it was needed.

For those of us who consistently had our boundaries crossed as children, all of this can feel very hard. We didn't have the physical ability, logic, or voice to express our boundaries then, and the belief that we can't do it might remain with us still. It's important to remind ourselves as often as we can that we are *adults* now, and although we were once victims or dependent, we are no longer in that situation. The more we put these practices into action, the safer we feel and the more confident we become. Without realising it, our sense of worthiness increases as the mind and body can see and feel that we are doing the best we can to look after it.

Other ways in which we can cultivate self-respect are through nonverbal boundaries, such as the boundaries we place around our environment, the boundaries we have with the way we treat our bodies, and even the boundaries we have with social media (e.g., who we choose to follow and who we choose not to follow). Whether a boundary be verbally expressed between two people, or whether it be something you implement energetically or physically, its sole purpose is to allow you to feel safe. Keep that in mind whenever you are doing this work. Regularly ask yourself, *Does this make me feel safe? If not, what do I need?*

There will be times when a person or situation is much better left alone or removed from your life, rather than continuously putting yourself in a position of discomfort or pain trying to make it work. I see this often within abusive or toxic relationships where the other person is simply unwilling to come to the table and meet the other halfway. If you are in a situation that is emotionally or physically abusive, where you are not heard, or where you are punished for your authenticity, seeking help to remove yourself completely from that situation might be the best way of keeping yourself safe. As difficult as it might seem, staying in a situation that demoralises you regardless of your attempts to create healthy boundaries will keep your belief of not-good-enoughness well and truly alive.

Journal Questions

* How would I describe my ability to set boundaries? Where did I learn this from?
* How were boundaries displayed to me as a child?
* In what ways do I allow others to cross my boundaries?
* In what ways do I cross my own boundaries?
* Which communication style do I resonate with most, and how does it impact my everyday life?

* How would I feel if I could communicate more effectively about how I felt/understand better how others felt?
* Where or with whom would better boundaries and communication be the most impactful in my life right now?

Lesson 13

Listening to Your Body

We've looked at mental and emotional self-respect in the previous lessons, and over the next two lessons I want to share with you the importance of respecting our bodies and our spiritual selves. I really don't believe healing is achieved through just addressing one part of who we are, but rather happens when we look at ourselves holistically and address all four centres of the mental, emotional, physical, and energetic bodies.

So much of our shame can be directed toward our bodies. We find flaws in every nook and cranny and fail to recognise the very function of the body and its ability or sole purpose of keeping you alive. Without this body you would not be able to experience this life. You would not be able to smell your favourite flowers or taste your favourite food. You wouldn't know the feeling of a cuddle from a loved one or the joy that comes through laughter and dance. The miracle of our bodies is that they give us life. Isn't that enough?

Not only does your body give you life, but it also holds and tries to help you process all the experiences, pain, and trauma you have not yet dealt with. The physiology of stress, as you have learned, affects all the systems within us and, if prolonged, manifests into disease and illness. So much is stored within our cells as a means of protecting ourselves, but even our bodies have a limit. This is why learning to listen to it and respect it through lifestyle, diet, movement, and breath is fundamental to your journey of feeling whole. The purpose of this lesson is to help you appreciate the body you reside in and to understand the physiological impact long-term stress, shame, and anxiety can have on your entire being.

The same ACE study I wrote about earlier in this book found that a person who had experienced any of those ten ACEs not only had a higher likelihood of mental illness and dysfunctional encounters but also had an increased likelihood of a wide variety of physiological medical conditions, including these:

- Obesity
- Type 2 diabetes
- Cardiovascular disease
- Cancer
- Physical pain
- Fibromyalgia
- Chronic fatigue
- Hepatitis
- Nearly all sleep disorders (sleep apnoea, insomnia, nightmares, narcolepsy, sleepwalking, sleep eating)
- Reproductive problems
- Ulcers
- Digestive issues

- Fractures
- Shorter life span (especially if they had six or more ACEs in their score)

Pretty impressive list, right? When our body is stuck in stress (whether it be fight, flight, or freeze), it requires energy, nutrients, and specific mechanisms to remain in that state for a prolonged period. If there is no relief, the result is a lack of attention in other areas of the body, such as sleep, digestion, and hormonal regulation. The body favours the stress response, deeming other systems unnecessary until it feels it is safe again. Eating, sleeping, and reproducing are simply not a priority when your body thinks it's being chased by a sabre tooth tiger.

When our body is in such a prolonged physiological state of stress, it struggles to find homeostasis (a fancy word for balance). It becomes inflamed and, understandably, the manifestation of disease becomes more likely. There has been so much research now written about the link between emotional pain and physical pain. It's not a surprise that healthcare professionals often refer to stress as the "silent killer", as it's usually not until quite late in the piece, when a lot of the wear and tear on the body has been done, that people finally see the impact (and finally seek help). Luckily, however, just as our bodies can become imbalanced, they can find balance once more. The ability for the body to heal itself when given the opportunity to do so is quite incredible.

So how does stress affect the different parts of our bodies, and how can one start to become more curious about the messages of the body and what that may mean about the state of the nervous system? Below is a brief summary of a few specific bodily systems with an explanation of exactly how toxic stress or unhealed trauma can impact each area.

Musculoskeletal System

When faced with a threat (whether real or perceived), the muscles tense up in response. They do this simply to protect you from pain, injury, or death. One of the main reasons we carry so much tension in our shoulders, for example, is because it protects the most vulnerable and unsupported part of our body: the neck. When a stressor passes, the body returns to its resting state, where the muscles are relaxed and at ease. This resting state doesn't apply, however, for those of us who suffer from unhealed trauma, anxiety, or prolonged stress. Because we are easily triggered, we are constantly in a reactionary state, meaning that our muscles rarely get an opportunity to find relief. Over time this tightness causes a wide range of musculoskeletal issues such as chronic back pain, fibromyalgia, arthritis, fractures, tendonitis, sciatica, and more.

Digestive System

During much of my career as a nutritionist, I spent a lot of time researching and tending to the gut and the digestive system. Over the years, knowledge of how the brain and gut are interlinked has grown exponentially, and it would be wise, in my opinion, for all practitioners within the fields of digestive health or mental health to always consider the way the two are co-functioning, when devising their treatment plans.

When we are stressed, one of the ways our body tries to keep us alive is by slowing down the systems it deems unnecessary in that moment of survival. The digestive system is one of these systems. If you think about it, who has time to sit down to a three-course dinner when they are being chased by a bear? This is basically the rationale of your nervous system. To optimise the nervous system response, blood flow will move away from the GI tract to favour other areas that need it more in the short term, such as the arms, legs, and brain. The lack of blood flow to the digestive system means that nutrients don't get broken down properly; the mucosal walls of the gut become thinner; the junctions lining our intestines become more relaxed, letting more bacteria into our system; and our hunger and fullness signalling is disrupted. All these things can cause stress symptoms such as bloating, cramping, constipation, diarrhoea, nausea, IBS, and indigestion. Over time it can cause chronic inflammatory bowel diseases such as Crohn's disease or ulcerative colitis.

Even more important, however, is that stress has a direct effect on our microbiome—the hundreds of millions of bacteria that reside within the lining of our intestines. Yep, did you know that you are made up more of bacteria than you are human cells? It's wild. An incredible contributor to a person's good health, strong immunity, mental state, and genetic expression is thanks to a diverse and thriving ecosystem within your gut. Unfortunately, however, stress is one of the main culprits that can negatively impact the composition, diversity, and number of gut microorganisms that we so rely upon to remain healthy and thriving.

These bacteria communicate with an intricate network of nerve cells that are only comparable to one other organ: the brain. Hence the reason why many people refer to the gut now as the second brain. This nerve system (called the enteric nervous system) is hugely responsible for the way we feel. It also connects the two organs through the vagus nerve. We refer to this as the gut-brain axis as it is in constant communication with each. When this network is damaged or disrupted, it not only affects our physical body through lowering our immunity (our bacteria are responsible for over 70 percent of our immunity), but it also affects our mental health by causing us to feel even more anxious or depressed than we already do. A well-known study known as the forced-swimming test wanted to see whether the health of the gut of mice would impact their motivation and drive to keep swimming for survival when placed into water, or whether they would merely give up and drown. Scientists divided the mice into two groups and gave the first group a strain of bacteria known to be beneficial for overall gut health. Their findings showed that these mice not only swam for longer with heightened motivation but also that when their blood was tested, it contained fewer stress hormones than the second group, which unfortunately gave up quickly and demonstrated no motivation or drive to survive.

When stress is prolonged in the body, the continuous disruption to the gut-brain axis alongside the lack of blood flow to the system will have a significant impact on the health of our GI tract as well as the diversity of our gut flora. It also impacts the amount of serotonin (remember our happy hormone?) within our bodies. An estimated 95 percent of the body's serotonin is produced by the cells and bacteria within your gut, where it is hugely responsible for the effective communication and signalling along the vagus nerve between brain and gut. Not surprisingly, studies now prove that patients who suffer with either IBS or inflammatory bowel diseases also showed an increased rate of depression and anxiety.

A quick note on diet and your body

I'm not going to go deep into which diets work and don't work because I don't believe in or like the diet world. I have seen way too many people come into my clinic with anxiety and disordered eating issues to vouch for that industry.

What I will say, however, as a former trained clinical nutritionist, is that your body usually knows and will tell you what it needs, craves, and wants if you are mindful of it and listen to it. There is a difference between craving food because it makes us feel better emotionally and craving food because our cells are longing for nutrients.

Years and years of research tell us that highly processed foods increase the risk of disease and illness purely because they have the exact same effect on our body as stress does. They are, in essence, a form of edible stress. When we ingest things not designed for our body to handle, it becomes stressed from the inside out. It puts pressure on our entire system in its attempt to break it down and remove it from the body. Processed foods, sugars, chemical additives, preservatives, excess alcohol, packaged foods with weirdly strange shelf lives... all these things aren't normal or natural. They destroy your microbiome, inflame the lining of your gut, put pressure on your liver, ferment in the wrong ways, and just make you feel super shit. It's that simple.

I don't care whether you are vegan or vegetarian or whatever. All I ask is that you take time to understand your body's needs and how you can obtain this through your diet. Because your diet is something you *can* control, and it's essential to keep you alive. That's a fact. A diet rich in whole foods (meaning food in its natural form) will allow you to have a wonderful balance of all the "naughty" things, too. When you give your body what it needs, it has the tools to handle the odd thing it doesn't love.

A really simple way of addressing your needs is to work with an integrative doctor, a nutritionist, or a naturopath who has a realistic grasp on things, not someone who is going to force you down a route of fad dieting because it's "on trend". There will be the need for supplementation or medication at times, too, but in my experience, that should be a temporary aid in conjunction with appropriate adjustments to diet and lifestyle. Learn how to look after your body from the inside out, as well as the outside in. Get your bloods checked once a year. Do the things. Show yourself that you care. It doesn't need to be so hard unless you make it so hard.

Cardiovascular System

Being in a state of stress or anxiety puts a lot of pressure on the heart as the heart has to keep circulating the blood and oxygen required to maintain that level of stress. This heightened level of blood pressure alongside the increased surge of stress hormones can increase the risk for panic attacks, heart attacks, stroke, hypertension, and inflammation of the arteries and veins.

Reproductive System

Ever wondered why your periods go haywire when you're in a prolonged state of stress? Or why some women lose their periods altogether after trauma or in conjunction with eating disorders?

I don't want to go into the ins and outs of the endocrine system as it would possibly fill the pages of a whole other book, and honestly, unless you are really into learning about the body, it can be quite confusing with lots of long words to pronounce and remember. Put simply, what happens is that the endocrine pathway associated with releasing your stress hormones (primarily cortisol, adrenaline, and noradrenaline) exerts an inhibitory effect on the hypothalamic-pituitary-ovarian axis. This means that being stressed disrupts or stops the normal endocrine function associated with a healthy cycle. Long term, this can increase the risk of amenorrhea (lack of a period), worsen PMS symptoms, decrease sex drive, impact egg fertilisation, and increase the risk of fibroids and ovarian cysts.

Prolonged stress or depression during pregnancy can not only affect the physical development of the baby and increase the likelihood of postpartum depression, but the heightened levels of cortisol and adrenaline in the mother's system can also impact the metabolic functioning and cognitive and emotional development of the unborn baby.

So, why don't we pay more attention to these things? From my own experience, the unfortunate truth is that humans can be very blasé when it comes to health. "You don't know what you've got until it's gone" is a great way to sum up the way many of us are toward our bodies. We belittle them, punish them, pollute them, ignore them, and then when they finally can't cope, we freak out about it and wonder why. The reality is that most of the time, it's 100 percent our own undoing.

I think that if people could see what was happening inside them, as you can a car engine or a watch, we might act a little differently. When something is out of sight, it's too easy to forget about it. But when it comes to this topic, ignorance is definitely *not* bliss.

What I see a lot in my practice is the disconnection between mind and body. So many people assume the two aspects of one person are separate when, in fact, they cannot be disconnected from each other. People tend to live so much in their heads, never checking in with what's happening in their bodies. The issue with this disconnection is that we lose a vital mechanism that helps us overcome stress and trauma. That being the intuitive ability to *hear* the messages of the body and to respond to them accordingly to soothe ourselves. What I feel many people misunderstand is that the nervous system is not housed in the brain, it's housed in the body, and if we cannot tend to the body, it will be very hard to rely merely on *thinking* our way out of our discomforts. As you've already learned, the most effective way to self-soothe is from a "bottom up" approach, meaning to calm the body first and then tend to the beliefs or thoughts of the cognitive mind.

Clinical psychologist and pioneer of the concept of somatic experiencing, Dr. Peter Levine, has this to say:

"Regardless of how we view ourselves, in the most basic sense, we literally are human animals. The fundamental challenges we face today have come about relatively quickly, but our nervous systems have been much slower to change. It is no coincidence that people who are more in touch with their natural selves tend to fare better when it comes to trauma. Without easy access to the resources of this primitive, instinctual self, humans alienate their bodies from their souls. Most of us don't think of or experience ourselves as animals. Yet, by not living through our instincts and natural reactions, we aren't fully human either."

Somatic therapy (sometimes referred to as somatic experiencing) is a practice that enables you to get back into your body to attune to the messages it is sending you and to release stored emotions or trauma. Where a psychologist will work from the mind inward, a somatic therapist will work from the body outward. Both with the intention of helping a client find a felt sense of safety, peace, regulation, and, therefore, homeostasis.

I was drawn to somatic therapy as a modality for helping my clients purely because of my experiences as a yoga teacher. If you practice yoga yourself, you may be familiar with the sense of peace and self-connection that comes from an hour of inward practice and attunement to your body. Over time and practice, you naturally become much better acquainted with your body and can even find emotional release within certain poses and movements. You learn how to use your breath as an ally for self-regulation and support.

You become mindful, present, and your ability for interoceptive awareness heightens. Your body becomes a sanctuary which you then take with you everywhere you go. This is because the physical sensations of the body tell the mind whether it is safe or unsafe, and vice versa. As I mentioned at the start of this lesson, the impact of one system on the other is woven together like a fine tapestry, and by learning how to attune to both the mind and body, we increase our chances for remaining regulated and for the experience of stress to impact us in a healthy, short-term way, as it is designed to.

Psychiatrist and author of *The Body Keeps the Score* Bessel van der Kolk writes:

"Trauma victims cannot recover until they become familiar with and befriend the sensations in their bodies. Being frightened means that you live in a body that is always on guard. Angry people live in angry bodies. The bodies of child-abuse victims are tense and defensive until they find a way to relax and feel safe. In order to change, people need to become aware of their sensations and the way that their bodies interact with the world around them. Physical self-awareness is the first step in releasing the tyranny of the past."

One of the beautiful things about somatic work is that it can really help us find relief from our deepest core wounds or beliefs, especially those of shame and not-good-enoughness. Often we can't remember exactly what happened or where these beliefs came from, but we know how they feel in our bodies. Unlike talk therapy, somatic work doesn't require a person to think too much about what happened. It helps them simply tend to the felt sensation. Through movement, breath, grounding techniques, and bodily awareness, somatic practices empower a person with the tools to return the system to safety. Techniques such as pendulation (where a person is slowly guided from stress response to relaxation response) as well as titration (where a person is guided through a traumatic memory whilst noticing the body and regulating oneself with the story) become powerful ways in which a person can find healing. Done slowly and repetitively, the inner feeling of despair or grief or unsafety can transform into confidence and a heightened sense of self-worth as that person learns to trust themselves within their own bodies once more.

When I incorporate somatic work into my practice, I often encourage my clients to take a guided journey into their bodies and to become curious about the ongoings happening within. Body scan meditations can be a great starting point for doing this, too, and you can find many different types of body scan meditations through meditation apps or online. Noticing areas that feel stuck, sticky, or dark. Noticing areas that feel open, expansive, and light. If you move slowly through a yoga practice and really take the time to be mindful as your body shifts and moves, you will also be able to pick up on the language of the body and hear more clearly what it is saying.

Mindful Check-In

As we start to become more attuned to our bodies, we then incorporate the compassionate attribute of curiosity, asking inquisitive questions. Let's try it now as a mindful check-in.

1. Sit comfortably and remove any distractions.
2. Close your eyes if that feels OK, or turn your gaze downward.
3. Conduct a gentle body scan starting at your toes and moving up toward the crown of your head.
4. When you notice a sensation or an emotion within your body that feels unlike the rest, start to ask yourself the following questions:

- *What's happening within this space of my body? How would I describe it?*
- *Does this feeling remind me of anything, and if so, what?*
- *If this sensation had a voice, what might it say?*
- *What does this part of me need in order to feel open, safe, or at ease?*
- *If I send a nourishing breath to this part of my body, what happens?*
- *When I expand this part of my body with my breath, what happens to the sensation?*

- *Can I stay with this feeling and simply allow it to be there?*
- *Can I validate and normalise this sensation or emotion rather than making myself wrong for feeling this way?*

Take a moment to see how the intensity of the sensation or emotion has shifted.

If you're someone who has tried talk therapy and clinical approaches to psychology to no avail, perhaps somatic exploration could be a pathway for healing. I personally believe that everybody would benefit from being better connected to their body, and it's a core reason why I incorporate somatic work into all my online programs and therapy sessions. I believe a combination of both top down and bottom up approaches is what truly delivers the most beneficial results, and it's exactly what I teach my students who embark on their Coaching Certification with me.

Journal Questions

✳ Do I feel connected and safe in my body, or disconnected and unsafe in my body?
✳ Do I feel like I can trust my body? If not, why not?
✳ Am I kind to my body? If not, why not?

* What symptoms does my body currently present with, if any?
* Am I actively doing something about these things? If not, why not?
* If I were to focus on certain symptoms, pain, or sensations present within my body, what do I think my body is trying to tell me?
* What do these sensations need from me— physically, mentally, emotionally, and spiritually— to find relief?

Lesson 14

Authenticity, Detachment and Inner Peace

I believe that each one of us has a true, authentic self which is unburdened by life's trauma, stress, or attachment wounds. It's the part of us capable of love, kindness, compassion, courage, and curiosity. I believe that this part is always there within us. It's just that it is overshadowed or forgotten the more we get caught up in the limiting beliefs or emotional weight of our experiences.

The final lesson in this step of reconnection is forging a deeper bond with this authentic self or, as I sometimes like to call it, your higher self. So much of our not-good-enough story stems from our ego. When I say this, I say it with kindness, but for the most part, it really is just all in your head. When we are so stuck in our stories, attachments, dependence on status, or the material world, we lose sight of the beauty and wonder of life itself. We forget to be grateful, we lose hope, we become bitter, unkind, and we become lost.

Rising above the superficiality of our thoughts and our ego and finding intimacy with life again gives life a greater sense of meaning and purpose. We learn to see that getting so caught up in the limiting stories we tell ourselves isn't really worth it at the end of the day.

This idea of the authentic self and the premise that we can rise above our ego might be considered by some as a spiritual practice. Spirituality is a complex topic to talk about, and I'm not here to sway you to become a devotee to any particular form of spiritual practice. But I am going to invite you to broaden your horizon and at least get curious about your higher self and what your path toward self-actualisation might look like.

A big part of this book has required you to connect with your compassionate voice. This voice is the voice of your higher self. When you think about who you are when you interact with the people you love the most, that is your higher self. When you ask yourself how you wish to be remembered by others, that is your higher self. When you find yourself momentarily immersed in awe and deep gratitude for the seemingly small moments of life, that is your higher self. When your gut feeling or intuition is pulling you toward a certain decision, that is your higher self. Find that part of you and get to know it well. It will be your anchor and your guiding light whenever you feel the weight of your thoughts or your past burdening you. Just as we always have a seed of love that resides within our heart, we also always have access to the part of us who is wise, responsive, and who longs for peace. The part who knows what's best for you at all times. We can receive guidance from this version of us if we dedicate time and practice to forging a connection with it. There's a couple of ways we can do this, and one of them is via a particular type of journaling practice.

Exercise

CONNECTING WITH YOUR HIGHER SELF

This form of journaling takes things to a bit of a deeper level, so it may take some time to find your flow with it. Have patience.

I like to see this exercise as a Q&A session or a conversation with my higher self and my soul. Society tends to bash out who we truly are, and we change or adapt in ways that leave us feeling out of alignment with life and disconnected from self. This exercise offers a way to tune back in.

Try to do this practice after some type of meditation or even a movement session where you feel you have "dropped out of the mind" and created some inner space; basically, where you feel more deeply connected to yourself. I love to do it after a restorative yoga session.

As you move through this exercise, know that it *will* feel odd at first. Don't over analyse what flows through you. If it feels comforting and supportive, then that is all that matters! Trust what feels good.

Find some space that feels comfortable for you with minimal distractions. This means your phone is switched to airplane mode, and you are in a room that comforts your senses. If it feels right, perhaps you'd like to light a candle or some incense. Maybe play some meditative-type music in the background to get you in the flow. If you use essential oils, diffuse your favourite smell. If you love crystals, have the one you resonate most with sitting on you or somewhere near you. Whatever it is, set your space.

Start with writing about an area of your life where you would like to receive inner guidance. This could be

- a recent event or situation about which you feel confused or uncomfortable.
- a memory that keeps reoccurring and causing you discomfort.
- a big decision you need to make, such as a career change, a financial investment, or a decision about a current relationship.

Whatever it is, think about what exactly you wish to know from your inner guidance and write down the question.

Try to keep your questions quite open and broad. I like to leave room for whatever messages my inner self needs me to know.

Some examples could be
- What are my next steps?
- What action should I take?
- Should I wait longer or act now?
- What is blocking me from moving forward on this?
- What is the lesson I am learning from this?
- What do I need to know about this situation?

Close your eyes and breathe through any discomfort. Allow your exhales to be slow and long, and listen to that caring, compassionate voice that will soon come to the surface. Notice if or when your mind tries to intervene, and if it does, simply return your focus to the exhale and listen closer.

Without overthinking, put pen to paper (or fingers to keyboard) and just start writing. Notice what messages of support, clarity, emotions, or wisdom arise.

Another way of forging a connection with your higher self and your intuition is through the contemplation of messages from objects such as angel or oracle cards. The practice follows a similar series of steps, involving shuffling the cards whilst asking a question in relation to an area of your life where you may feel confused, stuck, or uncertain. When you pull a card it's always your inner wisdom and intuition that interprets it. It works as if the card is giving that part of you the permission to speak through you.

It's very common that people get completely disconnected from their intuition at a young age. But I believe wholeheartedly that you are always the one who knows what's best for you. You hold all the answers within you. You already know the truth. It's just that usually you're so disconnected and so scared to find that part of you, let alone believe it, because at some stage in your life, it was the reason why you were rejected, abandoned, criticised, or abused. It's always this part of my clients that I focus on getting attuned with and helping them develop a meaningful relationship with. I know I've done my job well when my client no longer needs me and trusts the wisdom within themselves.

For me, the goal of self-development is inner peace. I want my body to feel at ease, my mind to feel at ease; I don't want to be so caught up in life that I miss out on living it. Regardless of which religious text you read or which spiritual philosopher inspires you, there will always be a theme toward enlightenment, nirvana, samadhi, bliss, wisdom, inner peace... whatever you want to call it. And attainment nearly always involves some form of detachment from the everyday nuances of life. I first really came across this concept of detachment during my yoga teacher training about a decade ago when we were going through Patanjali's yoga sutras. The sutras are an ancient Sanskrit text comprising 196 verses, divided into four chapters that teach the theory and practice of yoga. And as I was navigating through them, I came across what is known as *abhyasa* and *vairagya*, which form two of the essential aspects or ingredients of a spiritual life.

Abhyasa, which loosely translates to practice, persistence, or perseverance, tells us that attainment of enlightenment or bliss must come from consistent action, consistent effort, and consistent practice. And vairagya, translating to dispassion, detachment, or indifference, tells us that we must do this consistent practice but have no attachment to the outcome of our efforts or to the falsities of the stories of our minds. On your yoga mat it would look like putting in the time, effort, and energy to be able to do a handstand without becoming attached to whether you get there or not. Sounds hard, right? I remember sitting in class that day reading this one paragraph over and over, trying to wrap my mind around how that would even look in daily life.

And yet it stuck with me... to the point that I even have it tattooed on my wrist as a reminder!

I'm not sure if the way I have personally taken it is how it was intended to be interpreted; however, what it taught me (and continues to teach me) is not to become too attached to anything because everything changes, and everything is impermanent. Our thoughts come and go, our emotions come and go, relationships and people come and go... Don't allow the impermanence of life or the unpredictable nature of life to throw you off the course of being a good human being. Stay with your practice and do so with utmost presence—which means to stop the fluctuations of the mind and the obsessions of the ego.

A lot of people hear the word *detachment* and think that it means we become aloof or disinterested, but I have found it to be quite the contrary. Becoming detached from what's ahead of us, or to the stories in our mind, or the worries of our future, allows us to be fully *here*. And when we are fully present, we become so much more attuned to our lives, and every moment becomes so much more precious. I would say that detachment is the opposite of aloofness.

When I was first explaining this concept to my yoga students a long time ago, I used the analogy of a bunch of flowers.

Imagine someone delivering the most exquisite bouquet of flowers to your house, bursting with colour, smell, and containing all your favourite varieties. You already know that flowers only last about a week, maybe two if you are lucky. And so you aren't attached to them being around forever. You hold no expectation of them to be anything more or less than what they are, and because you know that one day they will change, the way you treat them in that present moment becomes so intentional. You take time to gently open the wrapping, being careful not to break any of the stems by accident; you find the perfect vase to suit the height of the stems; you trim them carefully; and then you place the vase where you can appreciate them every single day. As the week goes by you tend to the vase, changing its water, smelling the new roses as they open up, and taking a little moment to admire them as you walk by. You don't judge the flowers or criticise them for changing shape or colour. You don't compare the beauty of a sunflower to that of a rose. Eventually, the flowers wilt, the leaves dry up, and you discard them, wash the vase, and put it away. You're not attached to the flowers or the meaning of the flowers because you already knew that their nature is to change, and you unconsciously already accepted that truth when you received them. To me, this is the definition of presence, persistence, and intentional action coupled with nonattachment.

So, what does this have to do with shame, perfectionism, and our feeling of not being enough? Well, these are all just stories we tell ourselves. You've seen how experiences shape our beliefs, and then our beliefs shape our thoughts, and our thoughts shape our actions, and our actions shape our reality. If two people can have different perspectives on the same thing, then there is no ultimate truth. If you think you're not good enough, but your best friend thinks you're the bee's knees, then you're not 100 percent correct in your stance as someone else has already expressed an alternate viewpoint that they also deem to be true.

So much of the "not good enough" thoughts, the disgust toward our bodies, the anxiety about what's happening 10 years from now...

it's all just fluctuations of the mind. Regardless of how you view spirituality, at the crux of it all is the ability to transcend these fluctuations, to honour a greater good, and to move toward a self-less, calm, and compassionate nature. The nature of your true self.

As you read this, I invite you to get curious about your own attachments, about the thoughts that limit your experience of life or love, and about the parts of you that feel the need to criticise you or worry about your every move. What would life look like and feel like if you could accept that it doesn't need to be this way? That perhaps you are just holding on due to habit rather than truth?

There is a lot of evidence and research around the benefits of practicing gratitude, especially when it comes to transcending some of the thoughts and limitations of the mind. To help restore balance, if you will. The science tells us that the act of being thankful—like truly thankful—is linked to decreased anxiety and feelings of depression, a positive effect on bio markers related to heart disease, a decrease in blood pressure, improved sleep quality, and a reduction of stress overall. And yet, many of us forget to engage in this simple (free) practice. In fact, just 15 minutes per day dedicated to your gratitude practice can be all it takes to notice a significant difference.

When I was working at the drug and alcohol rehab and we got on to the topic of gratitude, it was usually met with a lot of eye rolls. It makes me laugh even thinking about it. So many people had an aversion to gratitude, and many of them truly believed there was nothing to be grateful about at all. Nothing. It makes sense that they found solace in their addiction, doesn't it? One client comes to mind when I think about how gratitude can literally change your entire way of being and help you reconnect to your higher self. He was in his late fifties, grew up on a farm in Australia, and worked on the oil rigs. He embodied toxic masculinity. He was very negative and had zero time for conversations about positivity or gratitude, let alone spirituality. We all sat in circle one day, and I started the session by asking everyone to name one thing they were grateful for that day. Most people struggled, but everyone managed to find at least one thing—except him. He stood up to leave and I kindly asked him to sit back down as this process was part of his recovery. He begrudgingly obliged and said, "Look, there's nothing to be grateful for. Everything is f**ked. I don't want to do this stupid exercise." I didn't force him but rather continued with the session, highlighting the benefits of gratitude and the science behind it. At the end of the session I led everyone through a guided meditation practice, focusing on what it means to embody gratitude. Not just to reel it off like it's some shopping list you have to tend to. But to truly feel into *why* we are grateful. Gratefulness is not a thought but an emotion, which means it evokes a sensation within the body. Usually that sensation is one of warmth, expansion, love, and deep appreciation. You can feel it in your entire being. And when you focus on what life would be like without that thing, you often feel even more grateful for its existence. Toward the end of the meditation this client started crying and immediately left the room, ashamed of his tears (because "men don't cry"). I let him be and checked in with him later that day. He shared with me that his resistance to gratitude was because it forced him to look at the consequences of his addiction and how it had taken away from him the things he loved the most: his children. We talked about why he was thankful for them and what they had given him and brought into his life. He shared stories of their births and of their personalities and of how proud he was of them as their dad, even though they no longer spoke. The longer we spoke, the more things he shared about what made him thankful. It was like we had opened the floodgates. And the most beautiful thing about this process? His gratitude for his children reminded him of the father he wanted to be and of what was truly meaningful in his life. Of his values. Of his higher self. This became the driving factor for his recovery and ultimately for his ability to reconnect with his son. He found me on Facebook about a year later and sent me a photo of the two of them together, with a message which said: "I am grateful for this. I am grateful for rehab. I am grateful to you." And it's moments like that which make *me* deeply grateful for the privilege I have of doing the work I do.

If you also roll your eyes at the thought of practicing gratitude, I urge you to at least try it for a week. Just 15 minutes a day.

Exercise

A GRATITUDE PRACTICE

1. Start by finding a comfortable space where you can be present with your thoughts and your body.

2. On a piece of paper, write down something you are grateful for. This could be your body, your partner, your pet, a roof over your head, the health of your child... anything that you know makes your life easier or better or more joyful in some way.

3. Focus on that thing and close your eyes.

4. Ask yourself *why* that thing makes you feel grateful. What does it *feel* like to be around them? What would it *feel* like to not have them/it in your life?

5. Notice what sensations come up in your body as you connect with the reasons of why and how they evoke gratitude.

6. Stay here with these emotions and notice the impact they have on your breath, your muscles, your thoughts.

7. Repeat with another person or thing.

As we continue to explore the higher self and the attainment of inner peace, and without meaning to sound morbid, a practice that has really kept me grounded, grateful, present, and ever-evolving is sitting with the thought and meditating on the temporary nature of life. On birth and death and what happens in between. On how interesting it is that we all move through this world thinking we will live forever, denying that each moment is actually sacred. It's usually not until the unfortunate passing of a loved one that people say to each other, "We should tell each other we love each other more", or "We should really learn to forgive each other more", or "We should just enjoy life more". And usually we do for a moment, and then we forget again, and we allow all this noise to interfere with the reality of the fact that we're all here for a short and unknown amount of time. Shouldn't we at least try to make the most of it?

I don't know what happens after death, and to be honest I don't even know what I believe when it comes to this matter. Do we just return to the earth from which we came? Do we move on to another life? Is there a heaven and a hell? Beats me. All I know is that whatever we do, or wherever we go, it's not here in this body or in this life exactly as we know it right now. So, what would it take for you to try to enjoy yourself as you are? To put in the work and the effort to rise above your not-good-enoughness and realise that, in fact, we are so much *more than enough* because there is only one of you, in this one moment, experiencing life in this one way? Take a moment to just sit with that... It's so, so, so incredibly beautiful that you and I and everyone around us is literally one in eight billion. That's how unique we are.

If we take this concept one step deeper, we are not only unique, but we are all interconnected by a common thread that makes us all the same, too. This is the paradox. Perhaps the only one thing we have in common is the thing we cannot see—call it consciousness, call it your soul, call it energy—it's the life force that keeps us connected. I don't believe that pure energy judges, criticises, compares, or gets stuck in stories. The energetic force within you is more than your body, more than your thoughts, more than your emotions. It's shared with other humans, with trees, and birds, and fish, and your favourite flower.

And so, if underneath it all you and I and anything made up of energy are all interconnected... then, logically speaking, if I hurt me, I hurt you. And if I hurt you, then I hurt me. That's why I believe that when one of us heals, it naturally creates a ripple effect and affects everything around us. The more we heal, the more we rise above, the more we find compassion, and the more we learn to let go, the greater chances we have at healing humanity as a whole and possibly, just possibly, finding a more peaceful existence for ourselves and the generations to come.

When I came close to the birth day of my son (which is when I first started the draft of this book) there was, and still is, a profound desire for us to all create positive change for the future. To take responsibility for ourselves and stop passing the blame onto something or someone else. To live in accordance with our higher selves and to stop getting so caught up in the stuff that doesn't matter and that won't matter when we are gone. So next time you get stuck in a not-good-enough story, in your pursuit of perfect, in anger, or self-harm, ask yourself, *Is it worth it?* Considering everything on the broader spectrum, is this one thing, this one emotion, this one action that may hurt me or someone else, really truly worth it? Ask yourself if there could be another possibility. Another perspective. A different way of looking at things. Another behaviour that is more worth it. A way of being that is more aligned with your values and your true nature of open-hearted love and compassion.

Journal Questions

- ✳ What or who in my life do I take for granted and why?
- ✳ Where in my life could I be more accepting?
- ✳ When was the last time I truly connected with the small things in life and appreciated gratitude for these things?
- ✳ If I could let go of my attachments to thoughts, emotions, or people, who would I be, and what would I be doing?
- ✳ Where in my life would I like to be more present and why?

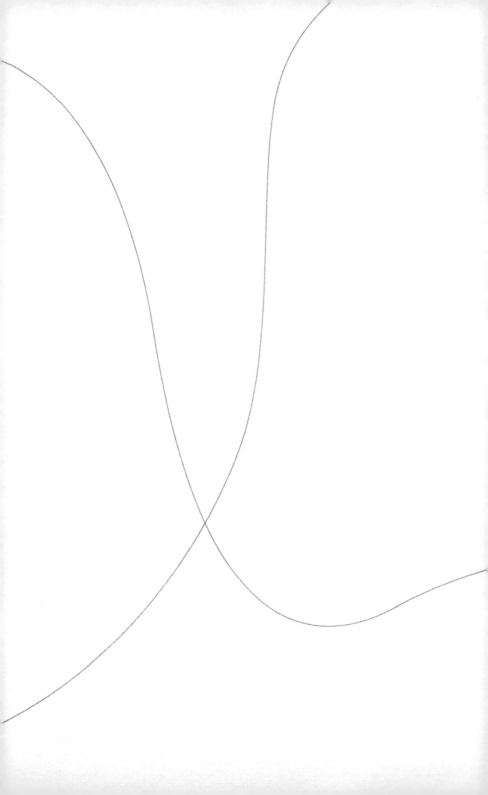

Step 4

Action

I truly hope that this guidebook has helped you broaden your perspective, consider new ideas, and perhaps even inspired you to consider how you might wish to grow or evolve in some way. Step 4 is not lengthy or too detailed. It only comprises two lessons, both around the path of *action*.

In Steps 1 and 2 we explored awareness and understanding, which are two crucial elements in the path of healing. As humans we are naturally curious beings and, therefore, we will be hesitant to try something unless we first *understand* why we are doing it. That's why it felt so important to me to spend the first two steps helping you understand your own story and the impact of that story on who you are now. To become the compassionate witness of your own experiences.

Step 3 focused on the process of unburdening—the practice of reconnecting parts of yourself to find self-acceptance and inner peace once more.

I have no doubt that some aspects of this book may require you to reread and rereflect to fully understand the concept of the topic, and I highly encourage you to do so. When we are new to the idea of change or healing, it can feel really daunting, and knowing where to start can be so overwhelming that we end up doing nothing at all.

That's why in this step, I want to speak about the ups and downs of healing and the natural back-and-forth nature of taking action. We'll look at why it's possibly the hardest part of it all and how you can stay on the path even when you feel like going backward is the easiest option. Healing is not linear, and it doesn't have a destination point. It's a continual evolution of oneself, going inward to integrate back into the world with newfound wisdom, clarity, and compassion. This is the step where I see so many people stop. Because taking action requires work, and consistency, doing things that feel unfamiliar and uncomfortable.

Lesson 15

Trusting Yourself

I cannot tell you how many times I have sat in sessions with tearful clients who have said, "But I haven't even progressed! Why is this so hard? What's wrong with me?" And then, when I invite them to reflect on where they were six months prior, they go, "Oh yeah, that's right."

The only time this isn't true is when they don't do the work required to progress. They don't take action.

As I mentioned earlier, taking action is the hardest part because it's the part that asks us to actually *do* something about our situation. Most of us love the learning process, but when it comes to actually having to change? Eeek! No thanks. Too hard.

I always ask my clients three things when this topic of self-trust and progress arises:

- What is the cost of staying exactly where you are?
- What is the benefit of changing?
- If the cost outweighs the benefit, then what is standing in the way of achieving it?

The greatest roadblock to your own self-growth is usually you. This is because changing is really, really uncomfortable. Fearing change is normal because it takes us into the unknown, and it's in the knowing and perceived control of things where we usually feel the safest. Not knowing what's next can send our nervous system into a frenzy.

Because of this fear of change, many of us choose to stay where we are. I see it all the time. We remain in toxic relationships, we don't quit the job we despise, we continue polluting our bodies despite knowing it's not good for us. It's not that we don't *want* to change, but more that we either don't believe we are worthy of it or that we have quite simply found a sense of safety in the comfort of familiarity and habit.

If you don't believe you are worthy of change, or if your habits and behaviours have become so comforting to you, then you might find yourself self-sabotaging any attempt to do things differently. Self-sabotage is usually fuelled by feelings of not- good-enough, and the more we do it, the more we perpetuate the belief that we are, in fact, unworthy of success or happiness or love. This is called negative confirmation bias. Any time we get close to change, we do something that will ruin our chances, and then we get to say to ourselves, *See? I knew you'd fail*, or *We knew this would happen. You're never going to make it.* And so the action or change never eventuates...

Another common reason why we self-sabotage is because we'd rather feel in control, even if that means we fail. It's almost like it's our way of predicting the future. We'd rather know we are going to fail and prepare for it rather than allow ourselves to run the risk of possibly succeeding. So many people do this in relationships: It's going so well, and the thought of possibly breaking up without knowing it's coming seems too painful, so we do it first just to be in control of what's happening (even though there is nothing fundamentally wrong with the relationship).

Taking the time to learn about yourself, read the books, listen to the podcasts, enrol in the programs, and do all the therapy is of no use if you don't use that information to shift things in your life for the better. In fact, what tends to happen if you don't take action is that you only become even more frustrated than you were before because now you *know* what needs to be done, but you still can't do it.

Action requires you to trust yourself and to show up for yourself every single day. But what does self-trust even mean, and what does it look like in action?

Before I answer that question, I invite you to reflect on a person you deeply trust. Someone who you know has your back no matter what. Someone who you'd call if things got bad. How do you *know* without a doubt that you can trust them? What attributes do they demonstrate that show you this is so?

When I reflect on these questions, the person who comes to my mind is my mother. I haven't mentioned her much in this book, and that's not because she isn't worthy of mention... quite the opposite, in fact. My mother was and is my guardian angel. My safe space. My nurturer. My childhood memories of her bring up feelings of warmth and comfort and unconditional love. Even when I was really scared or really upset, I somehow always knew I was safe when I was near her. I know without a doubt that I can trust her, through and through.

When I reflect on her and on the topic of trust, she embodies the following things:

- Congruency
- Reliability
- Compassion
- Clarity
- Honesty
- Safety
- Wisdom
- Validation

For me to cultivate self-trust, I must learn to be this person to myself. That means doing what I say I will do. Showing myself that I can rely on myself during times of difficulty or discomfort. Having compassion for myself when things get hard. Resting when I need to. Having clear intentions, goals, and values. Being honest with myself each step of the way. Keeping myself safe from harm as best I can through the implementation of boundaries. Listening to myself with kindness and compassion. Having my best interests at heart.

If I tell myself each day that I want to do something toward changing a part of my not-good-enoughness, and then I don't do anything about it, will I trust myself?

If I set goals for myself and then don't do any of them or sabotage my ability to successfully achieve them, will I trust myself?

If I blatantly lie to myself about who I am or where I am at in my life, will I trust myself?

If every time I make a mistake, I criticise and shame myself, will I trust myself?

If I knowingly put myself into harmful situations or allow others to cross my boundaries and create a feeling of unsafety, will I trust myself?

I'm assuming here that you answered no to all of the above.

Trusting another person is exactly the same thing as trusting yourself. It's just that the accountability falls on *you* to create that container for yourself. When it comes to the work of healing and growing, no one else will do it for you. And when you do start to show up for yourself and stick to your goals, practice self-compassion, and set boundaries, you will feel more and more empowered to keep doing the work. You will become more resilient. You will find so much safety within the crevices of your own skin. When you can trust yourself, taking action and entering the unknown is just not as scary as it once was.

One of the most common issues I see in the path of self-trust and taking action is that people try to do too much at once. They want to do the therapy, and the breathwork, and the yoga classes, and the green juices, and the hypnosis, and the past life regression, and the sound healing, and the list goes on... But it's just *too much*. As therapists, we are trained to move slowly with our clients when it comes to the implementation of change, healing trauma, or tending to new belief patterns. We must move responsibly, taking into consideration the person's ability to regulate themselves, their life situation, other stressors that may be going on, and their overall capability of "doing the work".

Creating an unreasonable to-do list that goes beyond our own capability will always result in failure or disappointment (it also has the potential to cause more stress than good), so it's important to take things slowly and within your realistic capacity to do so. A few small wins every day is much more effective than none at all, or one every so often. So as a little word of advice, set goals for yourself that are attainable, realistic, and feel comfortable to achieve. Meet yourself compassionately where you're at and move at a pace that feels right for you. Do this regularly and you will feel your life radically shift.

Journal Questions

* Do I trust myself?
* How often do I sabotage my own happiness or success?
* If I am being truly honest with myself, why do I do this?
* What about changing scares me?
* Where in my own healing journey am I not taking action and why?

* What small changes or small goals could I set for myself this week and this month that are achievable?
* If I trusted myself, how would my life look and feel differently? What would I do that I am not doing now?
* Who in my life can I think of who embodies self-trust? What qualities do they display?

Lesson 16

Trusting The Process

Many of us are perfectionists when it comes to our own healing journey. We make rules about how it should look, how long it should take, and what it means about ourselves if it doesn't go exactly as planned.

The truth of the process of healing or growing or whatever you wish to call it is that it is a *process*. It's a journey. And it's certainly not linear. Like any journey we embark on, there will be many setbacks, challenges, wrong turns, and unexpected mishaps. There will be times when we just want to turn around and go back to the place we once knew. Those moments are perfectly normal and perfectly okay. Truly doing the work is hard, and it doesn't necessarily end, either. Don't freak out when I say that. I just mean that once you start inquiring into yourself and peeling back layers, there will always be *more* to find, *more* to know, *more* to apply, teach, and integrate. There will be new depths to explore and new modalities to weave into your life. Each day you get to meet yourself more intimately and embody the most authentic version of you.

I remember my aunty gave me a card once when I was about sixteen years old that said, "If you're going through hell, keep going."

She was aware of how hard things were for me with my dad and saw me trying my best to hold it all together. And I did keep going. I kept putting one foot in front of the other, I kept inquiring, I worked with a therapist, I became curious about myself, and I stopped telling myself how the process should look. And I'm still on that same journey. It just feels different these days. It's more exciting as I know how to hold myself through all of it with greater compassion and understanding.

I will always offer my clients a little disclaimer to similar effect when they start working with me. That it's normal that you will reach a part in the process where it feels worse than when you started, but just *keep going*. If you can trust in the person guiding you, in yourself, and in the process itself, and if you can learn how to keep yourself safe and regulated during your journey, then you will be okay. It only feels uneasy because usually, when you start inquiring, you will encounter and unravel the pain that you have kept so well hidden or avoided for so long. We need to bring it to the surface and accept it to change it and the way we associate with it. Remember that everything is only scary if we tell ourselves it is.

If you are starting out on your journey toward healing and growing, I highly recommend that you work with someone you can trust. Do your research, identify what's important to you in a guide, ask lots of questions, and listen to your intuition. As much as insta-therapy can give us pretty pictures and snippets of wisdom, it's not until you are within a therapeutic relationship with a therapist, coach, or guide that trust, compassion, safety, and acceptance are truly born. An effective facilitator will teach you how to do it for yourself through holding space with you. They will teach you how to regulate your emotions and nervous system by demonstrating regulation themselves. By creating a safe container for you to express your emotions, they will show you that emotions are not to be feared. And ideally, they will give you tools and practices as I have done in this book, which you can practice integrating in your own time between sessions. I believe that a therapist teaches you what safety looks and feels like until you learn how to cultivate it for yourself.

As we near the end of this book I also want to stress the importance of finding balance between living life and doing the work of healing. Just like with any journey, you will take pit stops at a gas station to refuel, grab a sandwich, or sit in a park for a while. You will pull into a hotel to stay a night or two or decide to spend a few days (or weeks) really enjoying a new place you've never been. The same applies to this work. Please, please take the time to smell the roses and just be with life every so often. I think it's most beneficial if one can move in waves: Spend time on yourself in deep inquiry but then come up for air and allow everything you've learned, released, healed, and explored to settle into your life. Then, perhaps a few months later, you dive back in after having truly integrated the work of the past, ready to explore anything new which has arisen for you in that time.

The final thing I'll say on this topic of action and trust is that faith goes a long way. One of my greatest challenges has been learning to trust in something bigger than me, something I cannot predict or control. My nature is to want to know how, when, where and why... but sometimes we just don't have those answers. The reality is that the only things we truly can control are ourselves—the way we look after ourselves, the way we speak to ourselves and others, our thoughts, our actions, and our perspectives. Everything else is not in our hands. Like water, we need to learn how to flow *with* life rather than resist it and trust that it will take us where we need to go. As Alan Watts said, "To have faith is to trust yourself to the water. When you swim you don't grab hold of the water, because if you do you will sink and drown. Instead, you relax and float."

A personal mantra I repeat to myself daily is:

"I trust in things to unfold as they should. I trust in things to unfold as they should. I trust in things to unfold as they should."

And it helps me. If I think about it, every time I have leaned into trust, everything has worked out better than expected.

Journal Questions

✳ Where in my life could I lean into trust more?
✳ When I realise that not everything is within my control, how does it make me feel?
✳ What things in my life are within my control?
✳ What things in my life are outside my control?
✳ What would it look like for me to accept these things?
✳ What is the worst thing that I think could happen if I let go of control?

* How likely is this scenario to happen?
* What strengths and skills do I know I have that will enable me to overcome even the worst of challenges?
* What does faith mean to me?
* Do I have faith? If not, what could I start doing to cultivate more of it?

A Final Note on Honouring Your Gifts

B efore we part ways, dear reader, I want to offer you one more piece of information to contemplate. And that is that everything you have experienced has led you to where you are now, and therefore nothing should be of regret. The late Buddhist monk, peace activist, and teacher Thich Nanh Hanh famously said, "No mud, no lotus." Four words that are so profound and true. Without the darkness or the discomfort of your life, you wouldn't know the wisdom you know now. You wouldn't bloom into the person you are becoming. Someone once said to me that the universe won't give you what you can't handle. And although life can be painful, it's through the pain and through the "mud" that the gifts of our existence lie.

I invite you to take some time to reflect on the gifts of your pain and shame. The blessings that have been given to you as a result of your past. My past offered me independence, drive, empathy, a deep connection with my own heart, the dedication to find my voice, the drive to be a great parent, and ultimately my entire career and where I am today. If it wasn't for my past, I'm not sure whether I would have taken the path I did or whether I would be so dedicated to helping others. I certainly wouldn't be writing this book. I feel so purposeful in my life, but what led me here are the experiences I once found painful.

I've been in some pretty weird situations in my life. I've done things I'm not proud of. I've been in relationships that were extremely difficult and unkind. I've allowed myself to be used and abused on multiple occasions. I've put myself last. I've lied. I've been lied to.

And yet I regret nothing. If I were to look back at every single thing that was difficult, shameful, or hurtful, I could tell you what I learned from it and how it affected me.

There are always multiple ways of looking at everything. I could choose to look at my past with regret and shame and self-pity, or I could choose to look at it with the acceptance that it wasn't perfect but that it happened, and that the way it unfolded got me to where I am now, writing this book, being a mom, getting married to the love of my life, and living in a place where everything I desire and value is just around the corner.

Does it mean that my life is perfect? Not at all. I will still have things that frustrate me and make me sad. I will still be faced with multiple challenges and frustrations (hello, motherhood). I will fight with my partner. I will feel an incredible amount of imposter syndrome as this book gets published. I will make many mistakes. I will experience loss. I will feel pain. But I accept that pain is a part of life, and if I don't make it wrong or bad, it doesn't mean anything more than just a normal human moment in time. At the end of the day, I am a human. These things are all a part of human experience. It's how I choose to respond to these experiences of pain and the meaning I make from them that will impact me in the long term. And yes, how we respond is a choice we make once we have the awareness to do so.

With that said, I wanted to wrap things up by offering you my deepest gratitude. Thank you for staying here until the end. Thank you for reading the words that pour from my fingertips. Thank you for being curious about yourself. Thank you for acknowledging that you are bigger than your shame story. Thank you for being a part of the ripple effect toward a more peaceful world. I see you, honour you, and appreciate you so much. I hope that next time you feel unworthy or not enough in any way, you will be able to reflect on a part of this book, be it a word or a sentence or a topic which pulls you out of the funk and reminds you that who you are, as you are, is and always was more than enough.

Bibliography and Recommended Reading List

Below is a list of books and papers which have inspired me as a practitioner and were part of the research that went into the creation of this book. I have learned so much from these resources over the years, and I want to share them with you should you wish to deepen your knowledge.

- Archer, John. *The Nature of Grief: The Evolution and Psychology of Reactions to Loss.* Routledge, 1998.
- Brach, Tara. *Radical Compassion: Learning to Love Yourself and Your World with the Practice of RAIN.* Penguin Life, 2020.
- Brown, Brené. *Daring Greatly: How the Courage to Be Vulnerable Transforms the Way We Live, Love, Parent, and Lead.* Avery, 2012.
- Brown, Brené. *The Gifts of Imperfection: Let Go of Who You Think You're Supposed to Be and Embrace Who You Are.* Random House, 2010.
- Chödrön, Pema. *The Places That Scare You: A Guide to Fearlessness in Difficult Times.* Shambhala, 2001.
- Chödrön, Pema. *When Things Fall Apart: Heart Advice for Difficult Times.* Shambhala, 1997.
- His Holiness the Dalai Lama and Howard C. Cutler. *The Art of Happiness in a Troubled World.* Harmony, 2009.
- Hari, Johann. *Lost Connections: Uncovering the Real Causes of Depression – and the Unexpected Solutions.* Bloomsbury, 2018.

- Harris, Russ. *The Happiness Trap: Stop Struggling, Start Living*. Robinson Publishing, 2008.
- van der Kolk, Bessel. *The Body Keeps the Score: Brain, Mind, and Body in the Healing of Trauma*. Penguin Books, 2014.
- Levine, Peter, and Ann Frederick. *Waking the Tiger: Healing Trauma*. North Atlantic Books, 1997.
- Maté, Gabor. *In the Realm of Hungry Ghosts: Close Encounters with Addiction*. North Atlantic Books, 2010.
- Maté, Gabor. *When the Body Says No: The Cost of Hidden Stress*. Vermilion, 2019.
- Miller, Alice. *The Drama of the Gifted Child: The Search for the True Self*. Basic Books, 2008.
- Neff, Kristin. *Self-Compassion: The Proven Power of Being Kind to Yourself*. William Morrow Paperbacks, 2015.
- Nhat Hanh, Thich. *No Death, No Fear: Comforting Wisdom for Life*. Riverhead Books, 2003.
- Porges, Stephen W. *The Polyvagal Theory: Neurophysiological Foundations of Emotions, Attachment, Communication, and Self-Regulation*. W.W. Norton & Company, 2011.
- Sadhguru. *Inner Engineering: A Yogi's Guide to Joy*. Harmony, 2016.
- Schwartz, Richard C., *No Bad Parts: Healing Trauma and Restoring Wholeness with the Internal Family Systems Model*. Sounds True, 2021.
- Siegel, Daniel J., and Payne Bryson, Tina. *The Whole-Brain Child: 12 Revolutionary Strategies to Nurture Your Child's Developing Mind*. Random House, 2011.

- Smith, Julie. *Why Has Nobody Told Me This Before?* Harper One, 2022.
- Taylor, Jill Bolte. *Whole Brain Living: The Anatomy of Choice and the Four Characters That Drive Our Life.* Hay House, 2021.
- Watts, Alan. *Become What You Are.* Shambhala, 2003.
- Wiest, Brianna. *When You're Ready, This Is How You Heal.* Thought Catalog Books, 2022.
- Winfrey, Oprah, and Perry, Bruce D. *What Happened to You? Conversations on Trauma, Resilience, and Healing.* Flatiron Books, 2021.
- Wolynn, Mark. *It Didn't Start with You: How Inherited Family Trauma Shapes Who We Are and How to End the Cycle.* Penguin Books, 2017.

- Bowlby, J., & Ainsworth, M. (1992). *The origins of attachment theory. Developmental Psychology,* 28(5), 759-775. http://www.attachmentparenting.ca/articles/Bowlby.pdf
- Curran, T., & Hill, A. (2017). *Perfectionism is increasing over time: A meta-analysis of birth cohort differences from 1989 to 2016.* American Psychological Association, 145(4), 410-429.
- https://www.apa.org/pubs/journals/releases/bul-bul0000138.pdf
- Felitti, V., Anda, R. F., Nordenberg, D., Williamson, D. F., Spitz, A. M., Edwards, V., Koss, M.P., & Marks, J. S. (1998).

Relationship of childhood abuse and household dysfunction to many of the leading causes of death in adults: The adverse childhood experiences (ACE) study. *American Journal of Preventative Medicine, 14*(4), 245-258. https://www.ajpmonline.org/action/showPdf?pii=S0749-3797%2898%2900017-8

- Hewitt, P. L., & Flett, G. L. (1991). *Perfectionism in the self and social contexts: Conceptualization, assessment, and association with psychopathology. Journal of Personality and Social Psychology, 60*(3), 456-470. https://hewittlab.sites.olt.ubc.ca/files/2014/11/Hewitt-Flett-1991-Perfectionism-in-the-self-and-social-contexts-conceptualization-assessment-and-association-with-psychopathology.pdf

- *Dr. Kristin Neff's Website.* Self-Compassion.org.

Acknowledgements

This book has been a labour of love, born during a transformative period of my life. As I reflect on the journey from its inception, when I was six months pregnant with my son, to its publication, with him now nearly two and a half years old, I am filled with gratitude for the dedication, time, and commitment that have gone into its creation. Alongside these efforts, I've navigated moments of doubt and questioned my own self-worth, each time a reminder of why I wanted to write the book in the first place.

I am profoundly aware that my journey is woven from the experiences of my unique history, family dynamics, and my own version of trauma. Although some aspects of my upbringing presented challenges, I recognise how they have ultimately contributed to my evolution, offering wisdom and healing that have paved the way for this book. It is through embracing and integrating these parts of my story that I have found my voice and purpose and to which I can look back on my life in deep gratitude for its learnings.

I made a pivotal decision to change publishers midway through this journey, which proved to be one of the best decisions I've ever made. I want to extend my deepest gratitude to my editor, whose guidance and insight have been instrumental in shaping this book into its truest form. Your unwavering support and encouragement to infuse more of myself into these pages have been transformative, and I am profoundly grateful for your understanding and guidance.

To my clients, whose stories and experiences have inspired the case studies within these pages, I offer my heartfelt thanks. Albeit me being their therapist, they are the ones who continually remind me of the boundless capacity for change, compassion, and healing that resides within each of us. It is their courage and resilience that fuel my passion for this work and reaffirm my belief in the transformative power of self-development.

Finally, to my incredible family—my parents, siblings, and my husband—I owe an immeasurable debt of gratitude. Your unconditional belief, support, and encouragement have been a constant source of strength and reassurance. You provide the backdrop of safety and love against which I can weather any storm of self-doubt, and for that, I am forever grateful.

About
the Author

Nikki Heyder is a holistic psychotherapist, therapeutic yoga teacher, coach, and mentor who has worked within the wellness industry for over a decade, helping women overcome their feelings of unworthiness and low self-image as well as training fellow practitioners in her unique approach toward Compassion Focused Coaching. Specialising within the areas of disordered eating, eating disorders, addictive tendencies, trauma, and anxiety management, Nikki believes that a holistic, compassionate approach that encompasses the mental, emotional, physical, and spiritual parts of oneself is the path we must walk down to heal, grow, and ultimately remember our authentic nature.

www.the-soul-institute.com

 nikki.heyder

About
the Publisher

The Dreamwork Collective is a print and digital publisher sharing diverse voices and powerful stories with the world. Dedicated to the advancement of humanity, we strive to create books that have a positive impact on people and on the planet. Our hope is that our books document this moment in time for future generations to enjoy and learn from, and that we play our part in ushering humanity into a new era of heightened creativity, connection, and compassion.

www.thedreamworkcollective.com

[O] thedreamworkcollective